Country Inns
& Back Roads

*"Why should not the New Englander
be in search of new adventures?"*
THOREAU: *Walden*

ALSO FROM THE BERKSHIRE TRAVELLER PRESS:

The Country Inn Cookbook
The Indian In Connecticut
True Stories of Old New England — Yankees All
Holidays Bizarre Cookbook
Once Told Tales of Old New England
Shop Drawings of Shaker Furniture and Woodenware
The Berkshire Traveller Resort Book

FORTHCOMING:

First Encounter: The Indian and White Man
in Massachusetts
Stockbridge: 1739 — 1973

Designed by Janice Lindstrom
Cover by Nancy Simpson
Scratchboard drawings by Janice Lindstrom

Country Inns and Back Roads

BY THE BERKSHIRE TRAVELLER

THE BERKSHIRE TRAVELLER PRESS
Stockbridge, Massachusetts 01262

ACKNOWLEDGEMENT

We are most grateful to the Early American Society for permission to use the painting on the cover by Nancy Simpson of Longfellow's Wayside Inn. It first appeared as a cover painting on the May/June 1972 issue of *Early American Life*.

Second Printing
IBSN # 0-912944-05-6

To Nancy B. Simpson

Contents

MID-WEST

UPPER SOUTH

LOWER SOUTH

FAR WEST

CANADA

PREFACE

This is the seventh edition of "Country Inns and Back Roads." It is difficult to realize that the first edition had 16 pages and 12 inns. It all started because I had to travel a great deal on business and I found more enjoyment and hospitality in what I came to identify as country inns. I was attracted to the idea that in a great many inns it was possible to sit in the parlors and living rooms with the other guests and enjoy good conversation. I might even have been able to borrow a book from their library. It was also important to me that each of the bedrooms had its own distinct personality and there was no danger of my awakening in the morning wondering where I was! Of course I was concerned with good food and atmosphere, but I particularly enjoyed the idea of being warmly welcomed as a friend on each subsequent visit.

Over the years, this book, which began as a pleasant hobby, has grown in size and scope, although the growth has not been forced. It was a natural step to become interested in resort and destination inns where my family and I could enjoy vacations and holidays of varying length.

There was never an intent on our part to write an all-inclusive book . . . . a complete guide to country inns. Each edition is the continuing account of my adventures in visiting and re-visiting inns all over the United States, parts of Canada, and, in the future, England and other European countries.

As each new edition was published, there were always exciting innovations and changes. I well remember the year we enlarged our borders to include Michigan. It almost seemed like the end of the world. Then there were the guest ranches in Arizona and a handful of inns in California. We had finially arrived at the shores of the Pacific!

In this edition we have included the stories of our visits and re-visits to 116 inns in 25 states and Canada. The name and the town of each inn has been included on the state maps at the beginning of each section.

And so the idea has grown — and with it a feeling of considerable responsibility. The volume of mail we receive indicates that many, many individuals are planning holidays and vacations around visits to these inns. In order to have a book that is of service to these people (we call them Berkshire Travellers), we feel that there are a number of things necessary. First, the book should be revised and updated each year. In order to fulfill this assignment, we feel that it is necessary to re-visit every inn almost every year. This keeps us in touch with each inn. Furthermore, when there is a change in ownership or innkeeper we frequently feel that an inn should be deleted from the current edition until the new staff have an opportunity to adjust to the community.

A number of years ago we found that the keepers of small country inns had little opportunity to communicate with each other about their particular innkeeping problems, although each one was a veritable fountain of ideas and suggestions. With the idea of greater communication among innkeepers, we invited them and their wives to join us at a meeting once a year. This has grown from a dinner meeting to a two-day seminar, out of which have come a great many useful ideas and innovations which are being shared by all of the inns. For example, each of them would be very happy to accommodate a guest who wished to make a reservation at any of the other inns.

The close association and conviction of responsibility to each other among these innkeepers is another way by which our responsibility to the reader is maintained.

We are often asked about the future of this book. I believe that it is self-evident that many people are most interested in finding this type of personal hospitality. In many ways the inns are personified by some 19th century attitudes concerning reliability, sincerity, warmhearted- ness and a genuine desire to be of service. I receive letters from over one hundred people every year who are in- terested in going into the business of keeping a country inn. Apparently there are many people who feel that keeping a country inn and sharing a considerable part of their lives with their guests would be an ideal experience for them. There is mail almost every day from people who have visited these inns and want to share their ex- perience, or who have visited other inns and suggest that they might be included in the book. As long as there are individuals who believe in sharing, we believe that the place of the country inn is well assured.

The Berkshire Traveller
April, 1973

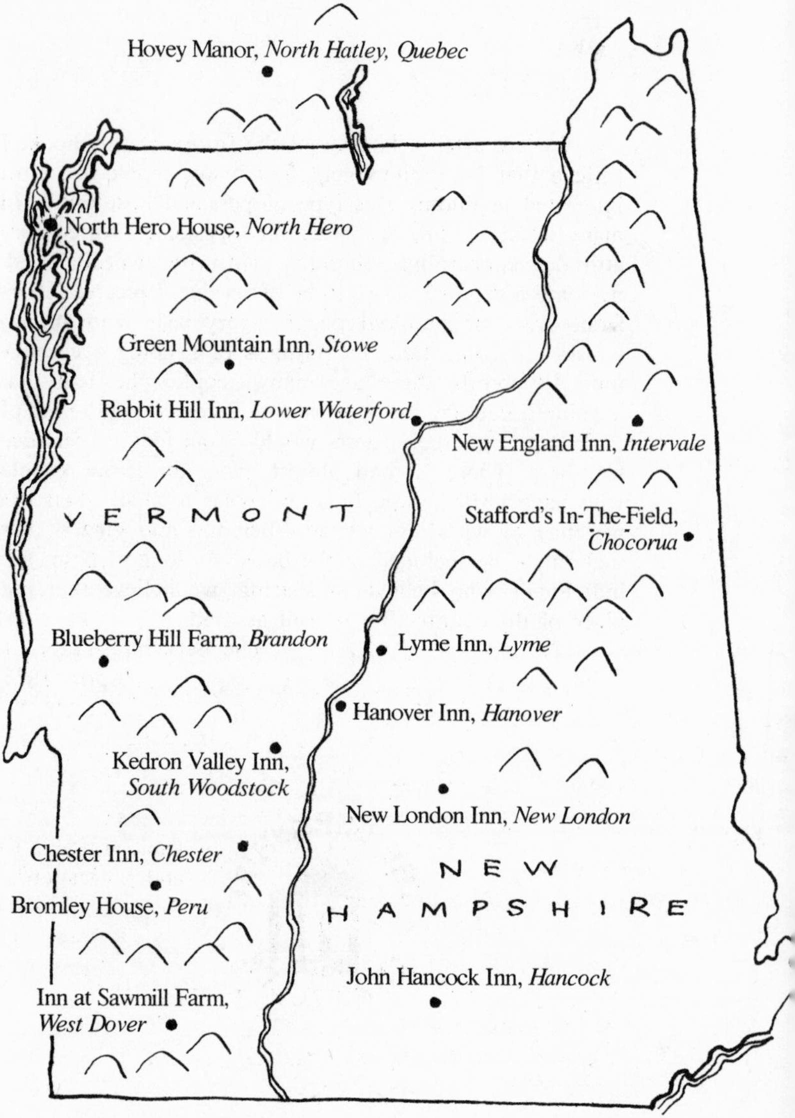

Hovey Manor, *North Hatley, Quebec*

North Hero House, *North Hero*

Green Mountain Inn, *Stowe*

Rabbit Hill Inn, *Lower Waterford*

New England Inn, *Intervale*

V E R M O N T

Stafford's In-The-Field, *Chocorua*

Blueberry Hill Farm, *Brandon*

Lyme Inn, *Lyme*

Hanover Inn, *Hanover*

Kedron Valley Inn, *South Woodstock*

New London Inn, *New London*

Chester Inn, *Chester*

N E W

Bromley House, *Peru*

H A M P S H I R E

John Hancock Inn, *Hancock*

Inn at Sawmill Farm, *West Dover*

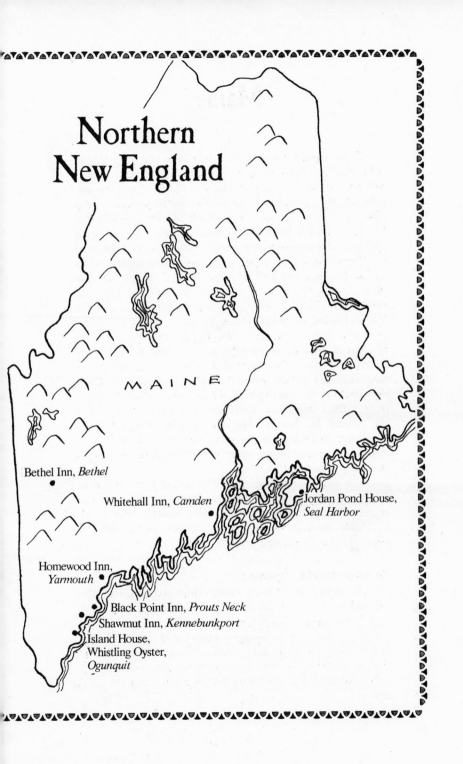

Northern
New England

MAINE

Bethel Inn, *Bethel*

Whitehall Inn, *Camden*

Jordan Pond House,
Seal Harbor

Homewood Inn,
Yarmouth

Black Point Inn, *Prouts Neck*
Shawmut Inn, *Kennebunkport*
Island House,
Whistling Oyster,
Ogunquit

Maine

From Boston I took I-95 which joins the New Hampshire Turnpike and crosses into Maine at Kittery. For a fast trip to northeastern Maine, the Maine Turnpike and I-95 will do very nicely. However, my stops were really along the coastline, so I went back to that old favorite, US #1. This follows the general contours of the coast and provides access to the lesser roads that lead down to the dozens of points, capes, and coves. The scenic routes off of US #1 are called Alternate US #1 in several places along the way. I traveled with the Maine map constantly available and spent many, many extra hours just following the roads down to places like Cape Newagen and Port Clyde. It is also fun to take a day trip to Monhagen Island. However, the passenger ferry is very small, and reservations several days in advance are necessary. US #1 passes through Rockland, Rockport, Camden, and up the west side of the Penobscot Bay, crossing over at Bucksport, and continues on to Elsworth which is the turnoff for Bar Harbor and Acadia National Park. However, there are dozens and dozens of roads leading down to several hidden coves and inlets between Bucksport and Elsworth.

I found the best way to get to Bethel from wherever I might be in Maine was to find Bethel on the map and choose the most direct route. Oddly enough, most roads in Maine seem to run southwest to northeast, and it is tricky to cut across the grain.

ISLAND HOUSE, Ogunquit

The three of us were clambering over the rocks to the Point where we could watch the fishing boats leave the shelter of Perkins Cove and head out to sea. Marge Laurent pointed out a string of buoys, and Paul was busy investigating several tidal pools. We sat down in the shelter of the rocks, and for a moment no one said anything. All of us were enjoying the continuum of earth, sky, and sea.

Finally I broke the silence (there's always someone) and asked Paul when he thought the ideal time to visit that part of Maine might be.

"Of course," he said, "Perkins Cove and Ogunquit are interesting places during our summer season, but naturally there are a great many people. I think the ideal time to come would be during the last part of May, any time in June, or during the six weeks following Labor Day. It's much easier to move around among the lovely old houses and all of the back roads along the coast, all the way from Portsmouth to Portland. We regret that we can't be open quite that long."

We walked back up to the inn, and I was struck by the unusual Van Gogh qualities of the myriad wild flowers that carpeted the Point down to the edge of the rocks. There is something completely sequestered on this point of land. I felt it as soon as I slipped through the small narrow gateway. It was formerly a sea captain's home and that atmosphere has been preserved. However, Marge and Paul have made it far more interesting with the antiques, paintings, and Americana that they have collected over the years. Every room has a truly exceptional view.

I was lucky enough, once again, to be able to have the "four poster room" for a single night. It has a high arched ceiling to accommodate the massive bed, and the feeling that I had when I awoke at dawn and lay there looking out over the ocean was truly wonderful.

Another of my favorite rooms is called "The Red Room", whose wall covering is a perfect background for its lovely, restful oriental paintings. It has a little balcony which it shares with another room, and an unobstructed view of the Cove, all the way to the sea.

After the Continental breakfast, which is served every morning except Sunday, I was taking my leave and Paul reminded me once again that the Island House is very small and it is best to plan reservations well in advance to avoid disappointment. I'd say that it is well worth the trouble.

ISLAND HOUSE, Ogunquit, Me. 03907; 207-646-8811. A seaside inn overlooking Perkins Cove, 15 mi. from Portsmouth, N.H. Lodgings include Continental breakfast served daily except Sunday. Lunch and dinner are not served. This is a tiny inn and reservations in advance are usually necessary. No children under 12, no pets. Open early June to October. (For lunch and dinner: Just a few steps from Whistling Oyster). Paul and Marge Laurent, Innkeepers.

WHISTLING OYSTER, Ogunquit

I can't keep it a secret any longer. I love Ogunquit — a splendid sea-girt town of writers and artists (and summertime tourists), good summer theatre, and browsable shops. I could while away hour after hour strolling the Marginal Way, a natural path which clings to cliffs high above the sea. More than my Berkshire Hills home-country, the ocean likes to change its moods quickly and decisively, from gentle splashing on a sandy beach to raucous waves breaking high over seaside rocks blending green, blue, and moody gray hues. It always brings out the poet in me.

By a curious coincidence, lunchtime arrived as my stroll brought me into sight of a restaurant just made for simultaneous sea-watching and dining. The Whistling Oyster! And there to greet me, the best baritone-innkeeper it has ever been my pleasure to meet, John Parella.

Had my meal not been so excellent, it would have been hard to keep from being totally distracted by the picturesque harbor scene framed by the wide, wonderful window-walls. I had settled for the seafood chowder, jumbo shrimp and mushrooms broiled in garlic butter, and a delicious sesame-seed-topped salad.

The service — all quick and courteous and efficient — was in refreshing contrast to the lazy and often circuitous courses that the fishing boats and yachts in the cove seemed to be pursuing. But for both sides, it was all in a sunny day's work. And, I was happy to be where I was.

After lingering over this seaside idyll, I poked through the enticingly well-stocked, adjacent gift shop and picked out a few new Christmas gew-gaws.

So I waved good-by to the Whistling Oyster, assuring John that I would be back again, and in fact I was — that evening for dinner.

WHISTLING OYSTER, Perkins Cove, Ogunquit, Me. 03907; 207-646-3334. A waterfront restaurant in Perkins Cove just off Rte. U.S. 1 at Ogunquit. No lodgings. Lunch and dinner served daily. Open Memorial Day weekend thru Thanksgiving Day. Reservations most advisable. (For accommodations: Just a few steps from Island House.) John Parella, Innkeeper.

Ogunquit Rocks

Cape Porpoise fishing shack

SHAWMUT INN, Kennebunkport

I was alone on a small concrete platform built over the rocks on the edge of the sea. There wasn't anything to say; it was all being spoken by the soft wash of the waves, the gentle August breeze, and by the changing lightshow being staged by the setting sun, the rising moon, the emerging stars, the sky, and the sea. The supporting roles in this production were being played by the red, orange, white, purple, and blue flowers in the twilight and the music supplied by the myriads of night birds.

Fulfilled diners were promenading the lawn. The placid waters of the pool reflected the lights from the porch and surrounding cottages. The deck chairs were neatly stacked next to the glass wind-screen, and the profusion of gay beach towels had been gathered up earlier by a crew of young attendants. The little red auto that brought the luncheon buffet to the pool was no doubt garaged, awaiting tomorrow's call. Some of the children were playing a last game of shuffleboard and planning a party for the next day.

Dinner had been a ball in more ways than one. It started with tender Maine shrimp, fresh swordfish moist in the middle and crispy brown on the outside, fresh green peas, warm cinnamon rolls, and frozen pudding. The American Plan menu selections were most generous.

At the next table a very young man was eating a mackerel that he had caught that day all by himself, and everyone for two tables around was joining in the kidding.

It had been an ideal day spent in the sun next to the ocean, with a late afternoon walk to admire the handsome Colonial houses of Kennebunkport, and a long walk out to the end of Cape Porpoise to see the fishing shacks and boats.

With the stars bright and the sunset spectacular, I could look forward to a similar day on the morrow.

SHAWMUT INN, Box 431, Kennebunkport, Me. 04046; 207-967-3931. A resort-inn on the ocean, 90 mi. north of Boston. Lodgings. Mod. American and European Plan. Breakfast, lunch, dinner served daily. Open all year. Frank Small, Innkeeper.

BLACK POINT INN, Prouts Neck

"One doesn't drive to the Black Point Inn," asserted the lady on the terrace, "One motors."

I believe that says it all. This genteel, Maine resort-inn is a throw-back to earlier times and gentler days. The composed pleasures include deft personal service by a most unobtrusive staff.

I walked out to the pool, encircled by gay blue and white umbrellas, in time for a very elegant luncheon buffet complete with a trio of musicians playing lightly in the background. Incidentally, in the evening there is music for all kinds of dancing, from waltz to watusi.

The many excellent tennis courts, the fine 18-hole golf course, and the white, sandy beach are actually part of a private club where inn patrons enjoy guest privileges. The same is true of the nearby yacht Club where sailboats are available.

Henry Petteys, the innkeeper, had a great story for me:

"One recent summer two New England Governors, guests of the inn, were asked to vacate the lounge at 6:30 P.M. because they were clad in sports clothes rather than ties and jackets!"

After lunch I was eager to stroll Prouts Neck once again and to see Winslow Homer's studio. The path goes around the Point with a stirring view of the sea.

Incidentally, here is an excerpt from a Black Point guest:

"We had a wonderful time there this year — everything, food, service, grounds, pool — was great. The staff was magnificent, Anne, John, Janet, Hubert etc. You have a great team this year. Hope it's the same next year — especially the weather! Please reserve Room #7 from 7/2 - 7/12."

I enjoy the Black Point Inn for all of these reasons. Like many devoted yearly guests, and many who are discovering it each year for the first time, I hope it never changes.

BLACK POINT INN, Prouts Neck, Me. 04070; 207-883-4311. A luxury resort-inn on Rte. 207, 5 mi. east of U.S. 1, 10 mi. south of Portland. Lodgings. American Plan. Lunch, dinner served to travelers. Open late-June to early-September. Henry and Mary Petteys, Innkeepers.

HOMEWOOD INN, Yarmouth

It was a neat little map. As he handed it to me, Fred Webster explained: "This is where it all started, the Maine House built in 1742, which is where the restaurant is located."

I walked past the tennis court, the swimming pool, and several of the eleven single and double cottages which make up much of the inn complex. A great many of them had fireplaces, and if not actually on the shores of Casco Bay, were just a few steps away.

I had been undecided earlier whether or not to stay in a small cottage with a deck over the water, or still another tiny hideaway for two on the shore right on the edge of the water. Many of the cottages would be perfect for a honeymoon.

"Oh yes, we have many honeymooners here," explained Fred. "In fact, they come back year after year."

I walked down to the sea wall which runs along the entire front of the property. It was poured by the Websters about ten years ago and has saved the land from eroding into the bay. Fred had explained to me that north of Portland is the rocky coast and south of Portland are

the sandy beaches of Maine. I walked out to the end of the long dock where there were rowboats and powerboats moored. Since it was low tide, in the distance I could see Seal Rock with dozens of seals sunning themselves. Later Fred took me out in the outboard, and they were tame enough so we could drift close to watch them in their natural habitat.

There are many things to do without leaving the inn property, including rummaging about in an old barn that dates back to the 18th century. It has a very attractive collection of antiques which are for sale. I enjoyed my stay at this seaside resort-inn immensely; it is worth noting that in a conversation I had with some people who live immediately adjacent to the Homewood, they reported that even at the times the inn was filled to capacity, things were always quiet and orderly.

HOMEWOOD INN, P.O. Box 196, Yarmouth, Maine 04096; 207-846-3351. An inn on the edge of Casco Bay, north of Portland. Lodgings. European Plan. Breakfast, lunch, dinner served daily. Open May 25 - Oct. 22. Fred and Colleen Webster, Fred, Sr. and Doris Webster, Innkeepers.

WHITEHALL INN, Camden

I came away from my first trip to the Whitehall Inn with a bulging portfolio of notes and two rolls of exposed color film. I also brought away with me much admiration for Ed and Jean Dewing and the Dewing children, Chip,

23

Jonathan and Heidi. All of the Dewings are very much involved as the new innkeepers of this old inn.

If ever an inn and a setting were made for each other, the Whitehall Inn and Camden, Maine are perfectly matched. The inn is really two buildings of somewhat similar neo-Greek designs connected by a harmoniously designed building in-between. It sets back from the main street, with huge elm and pine trees on the lawn. All three buildings are fronted by a broad porch, having window boxes and very gay summer flowers. Occasional arrangements of comfortable wicker furniture are just perfect for enjoying cool Maine days and evenings.

The first floor has a large lobby and lounge area, as well as several small rooms, all of which are furnished with beautiful antiques, and most of which have fireplaces. In the lounge area and on the porch are ingeniously converted sewing machine tables. In the secluded corners are chess sets which invite cogitation, jigsaw puzzles, an attractive collection of seashells under glass, and zillions of books.

Perhaps the most unique feature is the Edna St. Vincent Millay Room with an unusual collection of pastels of Miss Millay, starting when she was 18 years old up to the age of 58. There are several volumes of Miss Millay's poems, photographs of her, and among other things, her high school diploma. She was born in the Camden area. It was in the Whitehall Inn in 1912 on a warm August evening, so I am told, when a young Edna first recited her poem, "Renascence."

In the moments before dinner, which by the way was exceptional, Ed Dewing and I sat on the front porch directly in front of a little tree-lined lane that led down to the shores of Penobscot Bay where we would see several sailboats beating about among the green isles.

"This is a real change for all of us from our life in Boston," Ed explained. "We've all got a job to do, and it brings the family together. Jean's father is here and is always glad to drive a guest to the top of Mt. Battie, or sightseeing, and Jean's brother is our Resident Manager."

I'm certain that the Dewing's are going to make many guests comfortable and happy in the newly revived Whitehall Inn in Camden, Maine.

WHITEHALL INN, Camden, Me. 04843; 207-236-3391. A village inn in a Maine seacoast town. Lodgings. American, Mod. American and European Plan. Breakfast, lunch, dinner served daily. Open June 1 — Nov. 1. Ed and Jean Dewing, Innkeepers.

Ed Dewing told me that one of the Windjammer Schooners would be in port, so I arose very early and walked down the two blocks or so along the heavily shaded street with its Colonial-Victorian homes, to the harbor. All four sides of the church clock recorded 7:30 A.M. I saw dozens of cruisers and sailboats of various sizes from a wide variety of home ports up and down the Atlantic coast. This is a beautiful, sheltered harbor, and the gulls were already swooping for their morning meal. Some of the sailors were beginning to rub the sleep out of their eyes, tighten the lines, and swab the decks.

Behind the harbor are the Camden hills which are a sort of galloping geologic formation that come down

Schooner at dock

from the central part of Maine. The islands in Penobscot Bay are a part of this formation. In one corner of the harbor there was a cascading waterfall coming out of the hills, pouring beautiful, fresh water into the bay. On the public landing there were benches and trees, and already a few other curious folk like myself were taking photographs or sketching.

Camden is the home port for the Windjammer cruises, and sure enough, there was one of the beauties in the harbor. It was a most impressive sight. Some time I would like to try one.

JORDAN POND HOUSE, Seal Harbor

Charles Savage was explaining to me the noteworthy gardens of the locality during afternoon tea at the Jordan Pond House, the most outstanding probably being the Abby Aldrich Rockefeller Garden at Seal Harbor. However, two others are here, both provided by Mr. John D. Rockefeller, Jr., who likewise acquired and gave to the Park the Jordan Pond House where we were having tea, as well as the major portions of the lands which comprise Acadia National Park itself. The other gardens are the

Thuya Garden and the Asticou Azalea-Japanese Garden, both in the Asticou section of Northeast Harbor.

Charles went on: "The Abby Aldrich Rockefeller Garden is privately owned, but in recent summers it has been open for visitors on Wednesdays in July and August. It is a garden of great charm and includes numerous well-selected pieces of eastern Asian sculpture, some of which date back to the 7th century." At this point I made mention of the keyhole and moon gates and he explained that these also were inspired by Chinese examples.

Ancient Asian sculpture

The Thuya and Asticou Azalea Gardens are open throughout the daylight hours seven days each week. All have paths and pools. Flower displays predominate in the first two, while in the last more abstract designs prevail, including a Zen Sand Garden. These three gardens are only a few minutes away from the Jordan Pond House and occupy settings of variety and charm near these rocky shores of Maine.

As I looked at the attractive waitresses with their pink uniforms and sun-tanned faces I mused that if I were in college once again this would be a place that I would like to work during the summer time. However, that is only part of the attraction. The beautiful lake, the small mountains on the other side which are called "Bubbles", and the swooping gulls make it a summertime idyl. We were sitting under the trees on a very sunny afternoon in August; the tables were already filled with expectant and hungry vacationers. We were waiting for what is probably the most famous Tea in New England.

Some tables had been occupied since 2:30 P.M. Promptly at 3:30 the attractive college crew went into action, and fresh and steaming from the special ovens came the Jordan Pond Popovers! Such heavenly aroma, such divine texture! When we opened them to apply mounds of fresh butter, the sensation was enough to turn a strong man to tears. Then we piled on homemade strawberry jam. The fresh peach ice cream came later.

The Jordan Pond House located in the middle of Acadia National Park serves luncheon, tea, and dinner every day between June 16 and October 1.

JORDAN POND HOUSE, Seal Harbor, Acadia National Park, Me. 04675; 207-276-3316. A country restaurant on Park Loop Rd., 1 mi. out of Seal Harbor. No lodgings. Luncheon, afternoon tea, dinner served daily. Open June 16 — Oct. 1. (area lodging info: Acadia National Park; Bar Harbor, Me.) The Acadia Corporation, Charles Savage, Managing Director, Mr. and Mrs. John C. Sweet, Resident managers.

BETHEL INN, Bethel

Eleanor and Francis Callanan were most enthusiastic.

"As soon as we pulled up into that driveway underneath the awning, and saw all of that beautifully kept

lawn and those gorgeous flowers, I knew that I was going to love it," she said.

"I liked that nice veranda and the rocking chairs," explained Francis. "Whenever I see rocking chairs I know that I am going to find people to talk with, and that golf course out in back of the inn is just perfect."

This report on the Bethel Inn is part of a long chain of reactions that started in the summer of 1972. I visited this impressive old resort-inn at that time and was very much taken with the orderly atmosphere, bright paint, and high polish in evidence everywhere. As Francis Callanan said later, "It's like being on board a yacht that belongs to somebody with a lot of money."

Later that summer, while preparing the current edition of this book, I had occasion to recommend the Bethel Inn personally to quite a few people. The Callanans from Pittsfield, Massachusetts were among them. Now to top off the entire story . . . . in September I got a telephone call from Mal Jennings at the New England Inn in Intervale, New Hampshire, and he announced that he was going to be the new innkeeper of the Bethel Inn.

"Betty and I are tremendously pleased about the change," he said. "The Bethel does so many things that we both enjoy, such as fresh flowers in every room and beds turned down. You know, it's like the Black Point Inn in Maine or the Wigwam in Arizona."

There is much to do at or near the Bethel Inn, and many of the guests have been coming back for decades and staying for many weeks at a time. In an era when the New England American Plan resort-inn is on the wane, I find that the Bethel Inn, with its sumptuous bedrooms, parlors, and recreation rooms, is reversing the entire trend.

As Francis Callanan put it: "We're going back every year from now on!"

BETHEL INN, P.O. Box 26, Bethel, Me. 04217; 207-824-2175. A luxury resort-inn on Rtes. 226 & 5, 70 mi. west of Portland. Lodgings. American and Mod. American Plan. Breakfast, lunch, dinner served daily. Open June 6 - Oct. 14. Malcolm and Betty Jennings, Innkeepers.

New Hampshire

Do you want to get lost? Deliciously, romantically, bewilderingly but civilizedly lost, then go to New Hampshire. For instance, you can drive up Interstate 3 from Boston to Nashua and then head west into the Mt. Monadnock Region. If you throw your map away and try to rely on the signs that take you to Sharon, Greenville, Rindge, Fitzwilliam Depot, Dublin and Winchester you will have a wonderful time. You also won't be too far from a country inn in Hancock.

Now, find your way north toward New London and you can get lost in places like Newberry, Goshen, Wendall and Bradford.

In the Lyme area north of Hanover on the Connecticut River, it is a little more difficult to get lost because there are not that many roads going east. However, Route 10 north next to the Connecticut River as far as Woodsville has some great houses and up-country scenery. Getting lost in the Chocorua area is loads of fun. There seem to be dozens of roads that aren't even on the map, and you are never too far away to miss dinner at the country inn in that town.

From Intervale it is a good idea not to take any back roads west. If you are headed for Franconia, US 302 is the best answer. This is smack-dab in the middle of the White Mountain country and there aren't any other roads showing on the map. However, east from Intervale there are many roads trending into Maine.

THE JOHN HANCOCK INN, Hancock

I crested the last hill in the forest, and there on the staunch village street was The John Hancock Inn nestled among the other homes and churches and village common. I went through the old front door and there, with a big grin on his face was the new innkeeper, Glynn Wells, whom I met previously when he and his wife, Pat, came to Stockbridge to talk about buying country inns.

"Well, we did it and we are certainly delighted," was his comment. Pat came in almost at that same instant and the three of us had a good reunion. It was fun going through the inn again and seeing it all through their enthusiastic eyes.

When we reached the second floor rear room that has the handpainted murals, Pat seemed to bubble over. "This is a good bedroom, but we have plans to possibly turn it into a sitting room and a library, and thus allow all of the guests in the inn to see these beautiful murals which were done over 150 years ago, and have such a primitive innocence about them, don't you agree?" I did, indeed!

During my frequent visits, I have found the John Hancock Inn to be a very busy place. It is not only an ideal lunch or dinner distance from larger communities in New Hampshire and northern Massachusetts, but it is also in those deep woods that I mentioned earlier, which is ideal for vacations in various seasons of the year, including the famed southern New Hampshire autumn foliage. It is very close to southern New Hampshire ski areas and within a minute's walk of Norway Pond. Glynn also pointed out that many cross country skiers were also staying there this winter, because the woods were almost outside the door.

A very nice thing happened at dinner. Bearing my order of twin Tournedos of beef came the chef, Richard Doucette, who proved to be a very friendly and well informed man. He, in turn, introduced me to the assistant chef, Ralph Walter, and the two of them had a very refreshing enthusiasm for their work.

"Yes, I know we have a larger number of items on the menu than you might expect in a small inn," they said, "but we have a great many people who come back here several times a week, and the larger number of choices they have, the better."

The John Hancock is New Hampshire's oldest operating inn. It was opened in 1789 and I understand that Mr. Hancock, himself, never appeared on the scene, but because he owned all of the land they named the community and the inn after him.

I think that it is very fortunate that the John Hancock seems to have preserved the best of the past in both the building and its traditions. At the same time, its new owners, Glynn and Pat Wells, are bringing to it a great deal of enthusiasm and high regard for country innkeeping that ought to make it better than ever.

THE JOHN HANCOCK INN, Hancock, N.H. 03449; 603-525-3318. A village inn on Rt. 123 off Rt. 202, 10 mi. from Peterborough in the midst of southern New Hampshire's Mt. Monadnock Region. Lodgings. European Plan. Breakfast, lunch, dinner served every day in year to travelers. Alpine and xc ski. Glynn and Pat Wells, Innkeepers.

LYME INN, Lyme

The bell on the church clock sedately tolled seven times. Its tone was not obtrusive or raucous or insistent. It simply stated: "It's seven o'clock in the morning in Lyme, New Hampshire, and if you have business it's time to be up, if not go back to sleep." I went back to sleep.

I awakened about an hour later, and from my advantageous position in one of Connie Bergendoff's antique beds I surveyed the scene before me. It was, I conceded, the perfect bedroom and I would love to pick it up and transport it to the Berkshires! There were the matching twin antique beds immediately on my left. My eye caught a most inviting chaise lounge, a piece of furniture I'd like to have in my own bedroom. A fireplace, inactive now, but very much welcome during the chilly months, separated two side windows with a view of the inn carriage shed which the Bergendoff's have reconstructed for their expanding antique business.

The front two windows overlooked the village green of Lyme. The blue, flowered wallpaper harmoniously blended with the window curtains and the fabrics of the comfortable wingback chairs.

The Lyme Inn is a precise, antique-furnished New England gem. Bedspreads and wallcoverings, fabrics, furniture, paintings and the like have all been chosen to

successfully create a New England feeling. I must say here that I don't believe it is an ideal experience for children under twelve or thirteen, but it certainly is a satisfying and warming experience for a mature, sensitive individual with a keen appreciation of fine things.

Bruce, the young chef, who has been with the Bergendoff's since they acquired the inn 3 years ago, has enhanced his reputation with many innovations. I think his Bouillabaisse compares favorably with any I have had in New Orleans. He is also excellent with his fresh fish dishes. Imagine finding "first of the season" fresh seafood specialities like bluefish, striped bass, and shad roe at a New England inn near the White Mountains where the nearest water is the upper reaches of the Connecticut River! For those who prefer meat, he may be offering wiener schnitzel, roast lamb and beef fondue on his menu which he changes daily.

Although the inn sets on the edge of a long New England village green, it has a feeling of being rather remote. It is, nonetheless, just 10 miles from Hanover, New Hampshire, the home of Dartmouth College, and inn guests year 'round have the opportunity of sharing some of the sporting and theatrical events taking place at the college. It is also just down the road a few miles from the Dartmouth Skiways, an excellent ski area, and there is plenty of cross-country skiing nearby.

LYME INN, On the common, Lyme, N.H. 03768; 603-795-2222. A village inn on N.H. 10, 10 mi. north of Hanover. 2 miles from I-91, exit 14. Spring, summer, fall; European Plan. Winter: Mod. American Plan. Breakfast, dinner served daily to travelers. Dinner not served on Tuesday. Dining room closed last three weeks in April, first three weeks in December. Rooms available year-round. Alpine and xc ski. Ray and Constance Bergendoff, Innkeepers.

NEW LONDON INN, New London

The breeze off little Lake Sunapee was cooling and rather brisk as Frank Conklin and I walked up the beach. There was a clutch of sailboats involved in friendly competition, and Frank noted that it was one of the things that he wished he could do more often.

"Running a country inn," he said, "requires a great deal more time and dedication than most people realize, but we have a lot of fun, and Lois and I agree that it is really worth it. Now we have John and Betsy Banta as resident innkeepers, and I expect to have more time."

As I have pointed out in previous editions, Frank and his family came to the New London Inn a few years

Lake Sunapee

ago, by way of Deerfield Academy where he had enjoyed a long association.

"Lots of old Deerfield boys come every year," he asserted, "and I must say with a twinge, that their families seem to be growing larger."

Frank has a passion for accurate detail. Maybe that is one of the reasons I hear from so many of our readers about the good time that they have had at the New London Inn. As an example, the last time I stayed there I noticed that one of the twin beds in my room had a hard mattress and the other one had a soft mattress. There was particular attention paid to the way the beds were made and the linen arranged. This reflects its way right down to the picturebook living room and lobby where many antique chairs and tables are arranged around the fireplace. Frank and Lois have a way of putting everything in the right place, but somehow when they do it, it is more than comfortable.

"I know you are fond of kidding me about how I insist upon everything being just so, but it really pays off in our kitchen and in our food," he said. "I think we have the best cooks in New England, and we keep our kitchen so clean that we like to have guests come and peek in now and then."

Our walk continued, and he picked up a stray flat stone and skipped it across the surface of the lake. "This entire Sunapee Region has really opened up," he said. "People come to the lake for sailing, swimming and golfing in the summertime, and the ski areas bring many people in the wintertime. However, I'm happy to say that we have a great many guests who feel that they don't have to be active. They simply enjoy the atmosphere of our New England college town, and we find ourselves sitting around the fireplace on a cold evening or on the porch in the summer, telling stories and exchanging ideas. I think that this is the part of innkeeping that I enjoy the most.

"Another thing that we have are lots of walking and riding trails which are now used for cross-country skiing, as well."

The reference seemed to be a bit remote on this bright summer day, but the prospect of spending a few winter days at the New London Inn the way Frank pictured it caused me to make a reservation for January right then.

NEW LONDON INN, New London, N.H. 03257; 603-526-2791. A village inn in a college town 30 min. from both Hanover and Concord, N.H. via I-89. Near Lake Sunapee and King Ridge and Mount Sunapee ski areas. Lodgings. Breakfast, lunch, dinner served daily except Christmas. Alpine and xc skiing. Frank Conklin, Innkeeper.

NEW ENGLAND INN, Intervale

It was early, and I had felt comfortably cozy in my snug, little white-washed cottage. However, I was coaxed up and out with a reminder of all the things to be explored in the nearby White Mountains. Furthermore, I was persuaded that a dip in the pool was a good "waker-upper." It certainly was.

After that I was ravenous. Must be the good mountain air, because I had certainly put away hefty slices of roast beef at the inn the night before. Seated with Tim Porta in the cheery dining room, I scanned the breakfast menu. How long had it been since I had been con-

New Hampshire covered bridge

fronted with a choice of porridge with brown sugar (labeled north country style), country fresh eggs, buttered griddle cakes with pure maple syrup? There were two more splendid notes on the menu: hot muffins and donuts baked fresh each morning, and the inn's own special blend of coffee!

New England breakfasts are good examples of the old-fashioned Yankee tradition that the New England Inn maintains in this farmhouse-turned-inn 'way back in the late 1830's. The presence of so many of the younger generation is accounted for by the fact that there are so many things to do here. . . .like tennis and golf right on the inn grounds, or scaling the mountain peaks in various lazy and unlazy ways: via Mt. Washington Cog Railway, the Gondola at Wildcat, or the Skimobile at Mt. Cranmore. There's also the "footmobile."

The ladies, of course, enjoy antiquing in North Conway and other nearby Maine and New Hampshire communities. There are many covered bridges such as the one sketched by Jan Lindstrom above.

Speaking of tennis, the White Mountains are indeed becoming a center for this most enjoyable of sports, and right in tune with everything, Tim Porta called me just before we went to press to tell me that some new courts were being added right on the grounds and there were several weekend tournaments during the summer. Ski touring and cross-country skiing are also very important activities at the inn. Incidentally, its park-like atmosphere with the tall trees and the Colonial cottages is beautiful after a new fall of snow.

NEW ENGLAND INN, Intervale, N.H. 03845; 603-356-5541. A resort inn 3 mi. from North Conway, N.H. on Rte. 16A in the spectacular White Mountain country near several ski areas and ski touring trails. Mod. American Plan (omits lunch). Breakfast, lunch, dinner served to travelers. Open approx: June 15 to Oct. 31; Dec. 20 to Mar. 31. Timothy Porta, Innkeeper.

STAFFORD'S-IN-THE-FIELD, Chocorua

"That," said Fred Stafford, "is Mt. Chocorua. The most difficult thing about it is how to pronounce it. The best way is to break it into syllables, Cho-cor-oo-a. There is a legend that an Indian Chief with that name was killed near its summit by white men. It's a rather fascinating one, and perhaps after dinner when we all gather around the fireplace, I'll tell the other guests as well."

Stafford's-in-the-Field (hereinafter to be known as Stafford's) is the inn at the end of the road for which so many people seem to be searching. It has a porch which runs around three sides and overlooks broad meadows which disappear into a distant line of trees. It sits on a

small hill on the edge of a New Hampshire forest. It has a long history of being an inn, but it is in fact, a farmhouse inn. For example, there is a huge classic New England barn which has been marvelously preserved and is, today, used for many fascinating purposes besides storing hay and housing animals.

View of Mt. Chocorua

It is unlikely, however, that any ordinary farmhouse has ever experienced the results of Ramona Stafford's cooking. On my most recent trip I learned that she was trained under a great chef, and among the things she loves to cook are lamb curry, ginger chicken, prime ribs, chili rellenos con queso, and spare ribs cooked in maple syrup — doesn't that sound inviting?

All of the desserts and breads are homemade, and this is where the Stafford's 19-year-old daughter, Ramona, joins in. These include cheesecakes, lemon cream cake, angel pie, raspberry torte and blueberry pie. One of the great blessings is homemade muffins for breakfast!

These are days when Stafford's is growing. During the summer and fall the inn and the surrounding area have all of the appeal of the unspoiled countryside. In winter, however, these same woods and meadows abound in well-marked cross-country and ski touring trails and the Stafford's sons, Hans and Fritz, are always available to help with the skis and instruction if desired. What a thrill of a brisk winter's morning, to walk to the end of the porch, fasten the skis, and be in the woods in one minute!

I have a letter from a gentleman in New York who visited the Stafford's last year and says in part: "From the moment we left the highway and saw Stafford's, I knew it had to be a beautiful happening. Fred and Ramona are incredible when it comes to hospitality, and as you stated in your book, Ramona is definitely a gourmet cook. Our whole stay brought back memories of long ago of visiting my grandparents in their big, old country home on the farm. It is an experience that I will long remember, and I would like to say 'thank you' for taking the time to add this particular place to your book as it is an experience that your readers should definitely not miss."

STAFFORD'S-IN-THE-FIELD, Chocorua, N. H. 03817; 603-323-7766. A resort inn on Rte. 113 between Chocorua and Tamworth, about 17 mi. south of North Conway. Winter Specialty: ski touring. Mod. American Plan and European Plan. Meals served to house guests only. The Stafford Family, Innkeepers.

Vermont

Backroading in Vermont! It almost seems to me that Vermont is a state of back roads. US 7, I-91, and Rte. 100 are the principal north-south roads, however there are many lesser roads such as Rtes. 22A and 30 which are great fun.

It was not until just recently that most of the roads were in fact, dirt roads. They're still to be found in many places, but I am always wary of them during the months of March and April, because many turn into quagmires after the snow starts to melt.

Although the inns in this section are arranged in an informal circle tour, it is possible to put the map of Vermont on the wall and stand about ten feet away and throw a dart at it. Wherever it lands is a good place to search out and visit. One of these country inns will not be too far away.

INN AT SAWMILL FARM, West Dover

It was a soft summer evening with the moon a fiery red platter rising directly behind the steeple of the West Dover church. Rodney Williams and I were seated on the screened-in portion of the terrace, and the flickering candles at each table revealed some very handsome people, many of whom were in formal summer evening dress. I remarked on this to Rod, and he replied that quite a few of the guests, particularly the ladies, enjoy the opportunity to wear their more glamorous summer prints.

"I think it sort of goes with the menu," he asserted.

Running my eyes down the menu which did, indeed, include quite a few glamorous choices, I had to agree. It didn't seem exactly appropriate to be eating such delicately prepared dishes unless one were dressed for the part!

I find that there is a "key" to every country inn. Maybe this is the key to the Inn at Sawmill Farm. It has a harmonious blending of the textures of beautifully weathered barnsiding, brick, stone, drapes, carpeting, and

very impressive furniture and furnishings all mixed and matched with consumate decorating skill. They seem to bring out the latent tastes and enthusiasm of the guests. As I looked around, all of us seemed to sparkle not only in appearance, but in conversation as well. It must be the setting.

The inn is a group of elegantly fashioned farm buildings and a farm house grouped around an attractive swimming pool on a slight elevation overlooking the village. Rodney and Ione Williams came here about six years ago, leaving their interior decorating and architectural businesses in Atlantic City, but bringing many years of preference and expression to the country, and instilling them in this elegant little inn. The inn has grown and justifiably prospered over the years with many new buildings being added, and even a pond. Rodney said that the most satisfying development has been the addition of his son, Bill, who is now the chef.

As we talked on in the ever-growing darkness, there lifted up from the village below the most marvelous sound of church bells. Rod explained that it was the Special Deacon's Meeting which is held once a year. The first bell was a fifteen minute warning, and then a quarter of an hour later came the final call to the Meeting. It was an indication that although there had been many changes in this little Vermont village over the past few years, there were, gratifyingly enough, some things that remained the same.

INN AT SAWMILL FARM, Box 8, West Dover, Vt. 05356; 802-464-8131. A country resort-inn on Rt. 100 within sight of Mt. Snow ski area, 22 mi. from both Bennington and Brattleboro. Lodgings. Mod. American Plan. Breakfast and dinner served daily except Wednesday. Closed Nov. 12 - Nov. 30. Alpine and xc ski. Rodney and Ione Williams, Innkeepers.

CHESTER INN, Chester

Jim Patterson and I sank back into the comfort of the big chairs in the main lobby of the Chester Inn and were talking about the fact that in the mountain regions roundabout Chester, maple syrup was still gathered by horse-drawn sleds, and the buckets were emptied by hand.

At this point a gentleman rose from one of the large couches by the fireplace and said, "I couldn't help overhearing you. Are you the Berkshire Traveller?" I wasn't quite sure whether I should admit it or not, but the pleasant smile on his face encouraged me to confess.

"Well, I just can't tell you how glad I am to meet you and how many pleasurable days you have given my wife and me on this vacation." It developed that he had stayed at the Lyme Inn and the New England Inn and was currently at the Chester Inn. He was then going down to the Stagecoach Hill Inn in Sheffield, Mass'tts.

"The Pattersons," he stated, "really have a lovely inn here. They made us feel comfortable as soon as we came in, and I must say that Mrs. Patterson's cooking is superb."

This comment about Audrey's cuisine is something that I hear very frequently. I paid a quick visit to her in the kitchen before the dinner rush hour started. There she was, looking as chic as ever, this time wearing a blue one-piece pants suit. We went around lifting up the covers on pots and sniffing the evening fare.

The Chester Inn is a very comfortable village inn in central Vermont conveniently close to lots of summertime activity as well as the famous ski areas. The building dates from the 19th century, but the Pattersons have com-

Gathering sap for maple sugar

pletely renovated the interior with some tasteful combinations of reproductions and contemporary furnishings. One thing I learned on my most recent trip is that electric alarm clocks have been placed in every room for the convenience of the guests.

The front of the inn faces the active village green and has a two-story porch with very pleasant chairs. In contrast, the back of the inn presents an entirely different aspect with a quiet, pastoral setting. There is an inviting swimming pool and many flowers on a green carpet of lawn. The day I was there, the Pattersons had erected a canopy from Pakistan, and it provided a most colorful addition to this up-country Vermont atmosphere.

I must say I share the enthusiasm of the doctor from New York.

CHESTER INN, Chester, Vt. 05143; 802-875-2444. A village inn on Rte. 11, 8 mi. from Springfield, Vt. Convenient to several Vt. ski areas. Continental Plan (lodgings incl. breakfast). Lunch and dinner served daily except Monday. Closed November; mid-April until end of May. Alpine and xc ski. Jim and Audrey Patterson, Innkeepers.

BROMLEY HOUSE, Peru

Route 11 in Manchester heads straight into the mountains, and when I crested the summit, there was the vast southern Vermont mountainscape stretched out as far as I could see in a panorama of green trees, blue skies and scudding white clouds.

On the north side I passed the red and white buildings of Bromley Mountain Ski Area. Looking in the other direction across the valley, I saw the ski trails of Stratton Mountain which were etched against a dark green background. At each turn of the road there was a new vista at which to wonder.

Finally the familiar Bromley House sign: "A Country Inn since 1822." I turned left through the tiny village of Peru, with horses grazing along the sides of the road and a small pond. The open door of a country store beckoned, and at the end of the village street — the Bromley House, in a sylvan setting of maples, which are a riot of color in the fall.

It has a noble red chimney and a porch on three sides with comfortable porch furniture, including welcome rockers. There are Bennington jars filled with flowers. Topping off the unusually tall building is a Widow's Walk, certainly an oddity in the Vermont mountains.

Carefully clipped green grass surrounds the Gothic building and extends into the swimming pool area behind. I noted that some orderly soul had carefully tidied up the low stone walls.

I found Jack and Janice McWilliams enjoying a mid-afternoon dip with their guests before starting dinner. They excused themselves a little early, explaining that there were a considerable number of reservations for dinner that evening. Apparently, we house guests were not the only people who enjoyed Bromley House fare!

The main dining room has old wood panelling, red check tablecloths, bentwood chairs, and a collection of

flatirons. An old public room has been restored with a much-used fireplace and aging wooden shutters on the windows. An old musket hangs on the brick wall.

My room was up some creaking stairs and I learned to lean to the right against the fall line. The Bromley House is an old friend. I've stayed there many times, winter and summer. It's always a joy.

BROMLEY HOUSE, Peru, Vt. 05152; 802-824-5511. A country inn with resort features on Rte. 11; 10 mi. east of Manchester. Adjacent to Bromley Ski Area and others. Mod. American Plan; mid-Dec. to Apr. 15. European Plan from mid-June to Oct. 20. Dinners served to travelers mid-June to Oct. 20. Alpine and xc ski. Jack and Janice McWilliams, Innkeepers.

BLUEBERRY HILL, Brandon

I stopped the car for just a moment at the bridge over the brook. The sign, "Blueberry Hill Farm" pointed to the left, and I felt as if I had really accomplished something by following Tony Clark's directions from the village of Brandon and had not made any mistakes thus far. It was here, however, that I had to make a decision. He had explained on the telephone that if there was new snow on the roads I should go straight and go around "the long way." If the roads were clear, I should make a left turn at the Civil War Monument in the middle of the woods and follow that road. It would be more direct, he explained, as city people coming up for the first time might be inhibited by the hill. It sure was an experience!

And everything else about Blueberry Hill Farm was an experience as well. Tony and Martha Clark, young, energetic and inventive, bought this old farmhouse about five years ago and after living in it for a couple of years decided to have what could best be described as a "cross-country skiing inn." Blueberry Hill obtained some fame about ten years ago as an inn, but had not been operated as one for some time.

Here in the beautiful Green Mountains of Vermont cross-country skiing is just about everything. On the day of my visit it was cold; I mean really cold. Nevertheless the inn guests were out on the trails in full force, and every once in awhile a group of them would ski into the little rustic lodge where Martha keeps two tremendous kettles of soup on the pot bellied stove for anyone who needs to be warmed. Most everyone did.

The ski touring enthusiast is of a breed set apart and certainly has nothing to do with uphill lifts and other paraphernalia of the alpine skier. I believe Tony said there were forty miles of trails, "although you do not have to go very far into the woods to enjoy yourself." Skis, boots and poles are for rent at the shop.

The inn itself is very definitely family-style. Everyone sits around the big dining room table, and there is one main dish for each meal which Martha cooks in the farmhouse kitchen. This main dish is likely to be something quite unusual, as she is sort of a country cook with gourmet tendencies.

The rooms are plain and simple. . . . .it is very much like visiting an old farm in the Vermont mountains.

Blueberry Hill is closed during July and August. However, Tony says that even when there is no snow on the ground, guests are welcome, (especially if they want to come up and clear trails and maybe cut brush before the start of the next winter season.)

Children take to cross-country skiing most readily, although I think that Timothy Clark had a lot to do with fanning the enthusiasm of the young novices. Even Christopher, who is only 3 years old, was out on his skis.

BLUEBERRY HILL FARM, RFD #3, Brandon, Vt. 05733; 802-247-6735. A mountain inn passionately devoted to cross-country skiing. Off Rte. 73, 8 mi. from Brandon. (Phone for directions from the village.) Open from September to June. Closed Christmas Day. Mod. American Plan only. Meals not served to travelers. Tony and Martha Clark, Innkeepers.

NORTH HERO HOUSE, North Hero

North Hero House is a small country inn located on North Hero Island in the middle of Lake Champlain. North Hero is about 1 hour from Montreal, Canada, and 45 minutes from Burlington, Vermont. The lodging rooms vary from "country inn traditional" in the Main House, which has been standing since the late 1800's, to the more contemporary lakeside accommodations. It is nicely informal and quite ideal for children.

While standing on the shoreline watching a group of sailboats round the point and head for the dock, I met Mr. Goodspeed. Mr. Goodspeed is the kind of man everyone should meet on their vacation. I discovered that he has summered at North Hero House for many years and is a wealth of information about fishing, sailing, the woods, local history, or just anything about which you care to converse.

Innkeepers Roger, his wife Caroline, and manager Jackie divide their innkeeping chores for 11 weeks each summer. The Sorg children, Lynn and David, also have their daily responsibilities. They enjoy keeping their guests introduced to one another and the guests are kept as busy or idle as they desire. Bicycling, sailing, swimming, snorkeling, fishing, outboard motor boating, water skiing, golfing, mountain climbing, or just reading and sunning are on the agenda.

Each year brings new improvements to the inn. This year, all the rooms in the main inn, North Hero House, will have private baths, and the restored and replaced second floor screened porch will give lakeside rooms an enjoyable view of both lake and green mountains.

As I returned to the beach area, a few of the chambermaids and waitresses were having a "once a-round the bay" on water skis before they had to get ready for Thursday night's delicious lobster picnic on the old North Hero House steamship dock.

North Hero House is beauty, informality, good food, new and old friends, and a wonderful place to return each year.

NORTH HERO HOUSE, North Hero, Vt. 05474; 802-372-8237. An old New England resort inn on North Hero Island in Lake Champlain. Rte. 2, 35 mi. from Burlington, 1 hr. from Montreal. American, Mod. American and European Plan. Open from mid-June to Labor Day. Roger and Caroline Sorg, Innkeepers.

GREEN MOUNTAIN INN, Stowe

I received one of the funniest letters ever from my friend, Parker Perry, the host at the Green Mountain Inn. The essence of it was his experiences with the state in adding ten more lodging rooms in the area immediately behind the inn. He illustrated the point that Vermont has the toughest environmental restrictions of all fifty states and proved the point well.

I first visited Green Mountain Inn in March of 1967, and it has been on my schedule every year since. One visit is always in the summertime, when I enjoy Stowe the most. It has a reputation for being a rather mad place in the winter, and this is justifiable because the skiing on Mt. Mansfield, Spruce Peek, and Madonna is first rate. But, it is in the summertime that I can really appreciate its peaceful, country tranquility.

At the inn I always start my day with a wondrous Vermont breakfast which includes sausage and is topped off with a piece of apple pie! Food is indeed an important factor at this elderly Vermont inn . . . . it was built in 1833. There is a great deal of emphasis on New England food . . . . hearty fare that includes pork chops, ham steak, calves liver, and many more. I have seldom seen a larger selection of desserts, and Parker never fails to remind me that deep fat fried foods are never served at the GMI.

The red-clapboard GMI is a New England village inn that "puts on airs". Dotty Perry is responsible for the most impressive flower arrangements — real in summer and dried in winter. There are ample books, many of

Green mountain by-way

them are gifts from guests. Air conditioning is never needed, and there is a blessed absence of mosquitoes.

When it comes to back roads, craftsmen, antique shops, and gift shops, Lamoille County has more than its share. The Stowe Area Association Office which is right across the street from the GMI has directories to all of these, as well as a complete map of roads and tours of the area. This includes 11 suggested circle tours.

I am glad that Vermont has such tough environmental restrictions, and I am also sure that now that Parker has gotten everything squared away, he would agree with me. It is a state well worth preserving.

GREEN MOUNTAIN INN, Main St., Stowe, Vt. 05672; 802-253-7301. A village inn on Rte. 100 in a Vermont mountain town, 36 mi. from Burlington, 6 mi. from Mt. Mansfield, Vermont's highest peak. Mod. American and European Plan. Lodgings. Breakfast, lunch, dinner served daily. Alpine and xc ski. Parker and Dorothy Perry, Innkeepers.

RABBIT HILL INN, Lower Waterford

Did I ever have a tremendous time on my last visit to the Rabbit Hill Inn! It fell on a Friday which is Clambake night, and the offerings not only included steamed clams and clam chowder, but a choice of steak or lobster.

It was a very busy evening, but I did meet several people who were traveling via "Country Inns and Back Roads," and I directed some of them to visit both the Homewood Inn in Yarmouth, Maine and the Whitehall

Inn in Camden, Maine, which I had visited a few days earlier.

John Carroll does all the cooking, and Ruth runs the front of the house including the newly remodeled gift shop which has several interesting New England items, including colored photographs of the "White Village" (Waterford's soubriquet). She explained that on Saturday and Sunday nights when the buffets are held, the gifts on the tables in the shop are put away, and replaced by platters of goodies such as ham, roast beef, fried chicken, Rabbit Hill's salads, homemade bread and desserts.

I had a late dinner so that I could join John and Ruth. However, while I waited there was a running fire of conversation with the other guests about where to go to see the best views and where to find the best back roads and the out-of-the-way antique shops.

This inn is located some distance up the Connecticut River valley in Vermont's "Northeast Kingdom." Many people who visit there write me that they greatly enjoy the relatively unspoiled quality of this part of the country. They like to visit the library across the street from the inn to take out books without a fee or time limit. Many also enjoy the beautiful Colonials on Pucker Street (which is the only street in town) with their white clapboards and green shutters.

Oddly enough, the Rabbit Hill Inn at one time was a manufacturing plant for sleighs and winnow mills. Sometime before 1850 the massive Doric columns supporting the two front porches were added.

Throughout the inn there are fresh flowers, candles, Currier and Ives prints, and many other personal touches.

Lower Waterford, Vermont

The Carrolls, it appears, are collectors, and the most exciting growing collection is John's chess sets. He has been adding to it continually. There are some boards already set-up as invitations for guests to get acquainted and play.

A word of advice to the casual chess player: John is the Bobby Fisher of the St. Johnsbury, Vermont district! I found that out in short order that evening.

RABBIT HILL INN, Lower Waterford, Vt. 05848; 802-748-9766. A country inn located on Rte. 18, 10 mi. east of St. Johnsbury, Vt. Marvelous panoramic view of the Presidential Range of the White Mountains. Lodgings. Breakfast and dinner served to house guests and travelers every day except Tuesday during the winter months. Dining Room closed Christmas Eve and Christmas Day. xc ski. John and Ruth Carrol, Innkeepers.

KEDRON VALLEY INN, South Woodstock

It was a fantastic coincidence. Without planning it, I found myself back at the Kedron Valley Inn exactly one year from my previous visit. This time I arrived in the middle of the day, and Paul Kendall and I drove on one of those great, dirt backroads to a point where the youngsters, including Chip Kendall, were on a fifty-mile horseback ride and would be having lunch again (see 1971 edition). On the way it gave Paul a chance to tell me about a few of the things that had happened in the past year.

"Well, for one thing, on November 21st we had a fire in our kitchen which nearly took the entire inn," he explained. "I discovered it around midnight, and we roused the local volunteer company. We were able to contain it, and would you believe that a week later we were able to serve Thanksgiving dinner although our kitchen area was completely wiped out? It was our neighbors who pitched in and really helped."

I couldn't help but think of how this very neighborliness was one of the strong reasons why I am personally so much attracted to country inns everywhere.

"It really took us to the 1st of June to get everything straightened out. Meanwhile, we developed the riding programs about which I spoke to you last year. When you come next year we're going to have our own horse stable and riding ring just a few steps from the inn. We'll have some twenty horses and possibly some driving rigs

as well. Then we will be able to take our guests on Vermont back roads in the real old-fashioned way."

I've known the Kendalls since 1966, two years after they bought the Kedron Valley Inn. Since that time there has been continued progress, as they have done over the interior of the inn, added new lodgings in a rather unique log lodge, dammed-up their pond and made a really first-rate swimming area, and have now gone into the business of maintaining horses. With the proximity of the Green Mountain Horse Association in South Woodstock, every year there seems to be more and more interest for both youngsters and adults alike in the trail rides and the different programs that are sponsored by the Association.

The lodging rooms at the KVI are clean and comfortable, not what I would call "fancy New England." The buildings are old with several dips in the floors. Like the Bromley House in Peru, it has a tendency to lean a little to one side. There is a kind of Calvin Coolidge spirit about the inn that says, "We're certainly glad that you came, and we hope you like us the way we are, because that is the way we are."

KEDRON VALLEY INN, Rte. 106, South Woodstock, Vt. 05071; 802-457-1473. A resort-inn 5 mi. south of Woodstock, Vt. Near Killington, Mt. Ascutney ski areas. American and European Plan. Lodgings. Breakfast, lunch, dinner served daily except Christmas and April. Lunches not served from November to May. Alpine and xc ski. Paul and Barbara Kendall, Innkeepers.

Southern New England

Williams Inn, *Williamstown*

Lord Jeffery Inn, *Amherst*

Morgan House, *Lee*

Red Lion Inn, *Stockbridge*

Yankee Pedlar, *Holyoke*

Stagecoach Hill Inn, *Sheffield*

M   A   S   S   A

White Hart Inn, *Salisbury*

Mountain View Inn, *Norfolk*

Kilravock Inn, *Litchfield*

Boulders Inn, *New Preston*

C   O   N   N   E   C   T   I   C   U   T

Country Squire, *Killingworth*

Homestead Inn, *Greenwich*

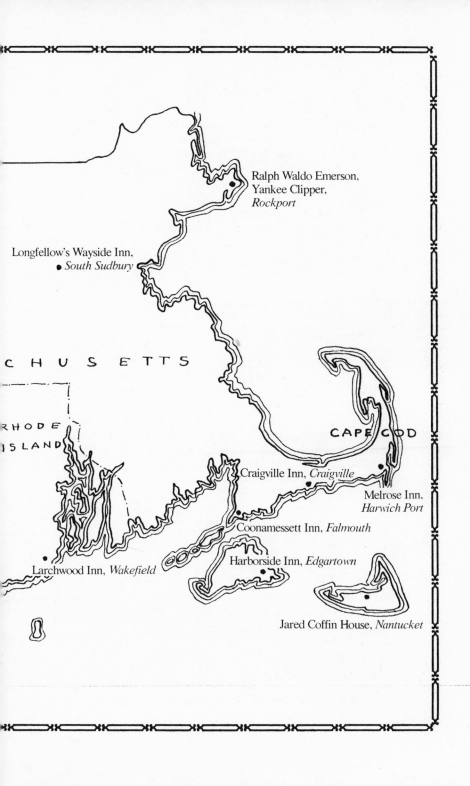

Ralph Waldo Emerson,
Yankee Clipper,
Rockport

Longfellow's Wayside Inn,
South Sudbury

C H U S E T T S

RHODE
ISLAND

CAPE COD

Craigville Inn, *Craigville*

Melrose Inn,
Harwich Port

Coonamessett Inn, *Falmouth*

Larchwood Inn, *Wakefield*

Harborside Inn, *Edgartown*

Jared Coffin House, *Nantucket*

Mass'tts

Long before the Massachusetts Turnpike became the principle artery from Boston to the Berkshires, Route 20 was the way to go. It was some ride then, sharing the road with the trucks. It is still possible to traverse the state on this road but I would suggest that the turnpike is best used between Ludlow and Westfield, thus eliminating the unnecessary traffic of Springfield and its environs. I would particularly recommend Route 20 between West Stockbridge and Westfield. It winds its way through some of the attractive hill towns such as Russell, Huntington and Chester. This is much wilder country than one might expect.

For an additional adventure, leave Route 20 at Huntington and follow Route 112 north to Route 9 at Cummington, or branch off at Worthington Corners on Route 143 through the Chesterfield Gorge into Williamsburg.

There are really no back roads from Boston to the Cape except an occasional alternate shore road as part of Route 3. However, once on the Cape, Route 6A which traverses the north shore through Sandwich, East Sandwich, West Barnstable, East Dennis and Brewster into Orleans can be a very welcome change from the main road through the center of the Cape, Route 6. This road gets you there quickly, but once you've done the first five miles, you've done them all as far as scenery is concerned.

In this issue there are new inns at Falmouth on the Cape, at Amherst in western Massachusetts and two on Cape Ann which is north of Boston past Gloucester. It is reached quickly on Route 128 and more scenically on Route 127.

One of the most scenic roads in Massachusetts is Route 2 west from North Adams. It twists through the lofty mountains in the northern part of the state through the towns of Charlemont, Shelburne Falls to Greenfield. This is known as the Mohawk Trail and so-called because the Indian tribe used this as a principle east-west path. There are several roads that lead off Route 2 into places like Zoar and Whitingham, Vermont. The scenery is almost alpine in nature and some of the views from the mountaintops are most rewarding.

COONAMESSETT INN, Falmouth

Everyone has played word association games. Someone names a place or person, and the rest say whatever comes into their mind first. When someone says "Coonamessett" to me, it's easy. I say: "Flowers," followed by "Food." This reputation for both flowers and food is well-founded. The Massachusetts Horticultural Society awarded the inn a silver medal for interesting planning and landscaping.

On my last trip to the inn, I made the acquaintance of one of those attractive ladies from Virginia, who seemed to know all of the flowers by their first names. "I've never in all my born days — not even back in Charlottesville — seen such flowers. Do you know that we drove all the way over here from Boston to see this inn?"

With tongue in cheek, I asked her if she was disappointed. "Disappointed?" she said, withering me with a glance. "Disappointed . . . . I'm thrilled!"

They invited me to pay them a visit in their two-room suite, and we sat on the terrace and watched the ducks. Her husband, something of a sportsman, seemed most interested in the different varieties. These Coonamessett ducks are well-known, and they're so tame. We had to pick our way through them on the way over to the swimming pool.

There are several different dining rooms in the Coonamessett, and I noticed that all of them were well filled for all the three meals served. The dinner entrees included Cape Cod clam chowder, regional specialities as baked haddock with a lobster sauce, fried Cape scallops, broiled scrod, baked stuffed shrimp and broiled stuffed lobster. If there is room left for desert, I always have the deep dish apple pie.

Meals are also served in the lounge, but there is a less extensive menu.

The town of Falmouth is on the western end of Cape Cod. It has some beautiful homes and churches and a very impressive village green. It is only a few miles from Woods Hole which is the point of departure for some of the boats that ply the Cape Cod islands, such as Martha's Vineyard and Nantucket.

One of the best things about the Coonamessett Inn is that all of this beautiful atmosphere—the attractive red clapboard buildings, the flowers and ducks, the enticing food — are available the year 'round. This makes it a wonderful place to get away to for a couple of days of rest and relaxation in the middle of the winter.

COONAMESSETT INN, Jones Rd. & Gifford St., Falmouth, Mass'tts. 02540; 617-548-2300. A Cape Cod country inn, 67 mi. from Boston. Convenient to all of the Cape attractions. Lodgings. Breakfast, lunch, dinner served daily to travelers. Clark Stailey, Innkeeper.

HARBORSIDE INN, Edgartown

It was 7 a.m. The mist on the Edgartown Harbor obscured Chappaquidick Island, and some of the stillness was shattered by one single "quack." A convoy of five ducks wheeled in and out of the Boston whalers and puffins moored in the harbor, but because there was not a single breath of air, it was as if they were swimming on glass. Each of the beautiful slim-masted beauties cast perfect reflections on the water in the pale light.

Mine was a room with a terrace directly facing the harbor, and as the light grew stronger I could distinguish the bright begonias, marigolds, roses, and lilies that were so cheerful and welcome on the warm September days. The pool which had been so inviting each afternoon, was now a dim blue free-form. A streak of golden light broke through the mist, and I knew that Arthur Young's prediction for a glorious day today was coming true.

I had big plans, including a sail in the harbor and perhaps 18 holes of golf in the afternoon.

There was something new in the air—the aroma of frying bacon. It came from the Navigator Room where preparations for breakfast were already underway, and where last night I had enjoyed a delicious dinner of scallops and king crab. The upper deck provides a beautiful view of the harbor which is particularly interesting at twilight as the boats are returning after a day on the waters surrounding Martha's Vineyard. Arthur had pointed out the sights.

Martha's Vineyard dock

The Harborside is a country inn on the water in Edgartown, which is on the seaward side of Martha's Vineyard Island. It is actually made up of several homes of former Martha's Vineyard sailing captains whose front doors were on the narrow quaint street and whose back doors open on to the harbor. I have always enjoyed a visit here in the fall because not only Edgartown, but also the other distinctive communities that make up Martha's Vineyard are more enjoyable during the leisurely first warm weeks after the season is over.

Now it was 8 a.m. and the island across the harbor was clearly visible. My original five ducks had been joined by several others, and they were a self-appointed inspection crew going from dock to dock and mooring to mooring. The sun broke through in full array, another great day at Harborside was truly underway.

HARBORSIDE INN, Martha's Vineyard Island, Edgartown, Mass. 02539; 617-627-4321. An island resort inn. Ferry from Woods Hole, Mass. Car reservations advisable. Lodgings. Breakfast, lunch, dinner served daily from May through October. Arthur Young, Innkeeper.

JARED COFFIN HOUSE, Nantucket

It's difficult to believe that this sturdily built, Federally dimensioned house is an inn. Only the discreet murmur of voices and muffled clinking of silver from a tree-shaded patio gives its identity away. It seems just like the other handsome houses of Nantucket whaling captains.

It was good to see Phil Read again, and I was very pleased when I realized that I was going back to one of the Crewel Rooms, with those splendid four-poster beds and the beautiful antiques. Interestingly enough, I have met three other people in my travels about the country who have also been guests at the Jared Coffin House, and were also put into these Crewel Rooms.

Nantucket Island, "The Little Grey Lady Of The Sea", is located 30 miles at sea from Woods Hole, and

Nantucket doorways

natives do, indeed, live here year 'round. During the summer and fall it is almost always necessary to make automobile reservations on the ferry. However, a car is not really necessary to enjoy the island to the utmost. A visit to the bicycle shop will not only provide wheels but also amusing diversion.

One of the most enjoyable seasons of the year is Christmas time. There are some quaint island customs for the holidays that have been carried over from the old whaling days. There have been many feature stories about Christmas on the island, and as a result it is almost always necessary to reserve many months in advance.

I enjoy just strolling about the winding streets, happily coping with the cobblestones, and bicycling out to look at the Scotch heather, wood lilies, and wild roses on the moors. These also provide a haven for rare birds such as the Swedish Nightingale and the Yellow-bellied Bulbul.

This kind of activity naturally makes for hearty appetites, and I particularly favor the Jared Coffin specialties such as Quahaug chowder and bay scallops.

Visiting Nantucket is always a unique experience. Staying at the Jared Coffin House is probably the closest thing that I found to actually feeling like I am a native for a few days.

JARED COFFIN HOUSE, Nantucket Island, Mass. 02554; 617-228-2400. Accessible by air from Boston and Hyannis. A village inn 30 mi. at sea accessible by ferry from Woods Hole, Mass. for which automobile reservations are usually needed in advance (617-426-1855). Lodgings. Breakfast, lunch, dinner served daily. Strongly advise verifying accommodations before planning a trip to Nantucket in any season. Phil Read, Innkeeper.

CRAIGVILLE INN, Craigville

The gentleman called out to me as I was walking down the Craigville Green toward the beach:

"Going for a swim — so am I, let's walk down together." He was a well-tanned, pleasant individual with a slight southern accent, and we exchanged pleasantries about homes, size of family, and length of stay. He certainly was enthusiastic.

"We've got a large family and we like it here because they welcome children instead of merely tolerating them." I had to agree to that.

We passed the tennis courts and left the village green with its restless pines set amidst the rustic lodges. The sun-washed buildings had the silver patina that is only found on the Cape. The sparkling ocean, the immaculate beach with soft sand was soon under our feet.

"Back home they told me it was the best beach on Cape Cod," he said. We both plunged into the warm, south-shore water and after about 100 yards rolled over to float on our backs.

"You know, we were a little hesitant about coming to a place run by a church, but it's the best vacation we've ever had, and we're coming back next year. And I'll tell you something else," he said, "back home we go to another church."

He toweled off vigorously. "I want to get back in time for dinner," he explained, as we started back at a quickened pace. "Boy, I've put on five pounds since I've been here." I pulled in my own stomach and tried to look slim. It wasn't easy.

Craigville at turn of the century

Author's addenda: Ever since I first visited the Craigville Inn a number of years ago and have included it in each edition of "Country Inns and Back Roads", I have received a gratifying number of letters and telephone calls from guests who find that a church-operated family resort-inn provides an ideal vacation.

CRAIGVILLE INN, Craigville, Mass. 02636; 617-775-1265. A resort inn with ocean beach. Also a conference center operated by United Church of Christ. 2½ mi. from Hyannis, Mass. Exit 6 Mid-Cape Hwy. Mod. American Plan. Breakfast, dinner served every day. Rev. Edmund Nutting, Innkeeper.

MELROSE INN, Harwich Port

There are some things that are perfect the way they have been for many years. I hope they never change. Apparently one of my readers from the midwest feels the way I do about the Melrose Inn. She writes:

"We found the Melrose Inn just as we left it the last time we were there, being run very efficiently. The meals are wonderful and everything is in marvelous shape . . . immaculate! Everyone was very kind and considerate to us. We were very happy to find the Melrose Inn today is still like the Melrose Inn of yesterday, which is a situation that I do not find very frequently.

"Thank you."

One of the things that I like about the Melrose is the great number of books available in the large parlor on the west side, and all the extremely comfortable chairs, sofas and braided rugs. It is always very nice to sit there and look out over the lawn bowling area. Even now I can hear the click of those wooden balls.

The Melrose is one of the few remaining American Plan inns on the Cape. It puts a great deal of emphasis on the rather simple joys: tranquility, privacy, sincerity, conversation, spaciousness and a most sumptious table. I kept my menu showing choices of stuffed shrimp, broiled lobster, sirloin steak, Cape scallops and filet of sole. There were also pork chops and calves liver. Pies, all homemade, included such New England favorites as apple, mince and squash.

In addition to the swimming pool on the grounds, the inn also has a very excellent private beach within walking distance, and swimming in the warm, south shore water is a delight on a warm summers' day. Also available to the guests is a new 30ft. launch for cruising, fishing or water skiing.

Cape Cod sand dunes

I think a word or two is in order here about Harwich Port. The village itself is very conveniently located so attractions or events at either end of the Cape are easily accessible. It is a community of rolling green lawns and an abundance of flowers everywhere, particularly roses. The atmosphere is quiet and restrained in a sort of natural way.

1973 will be the 53rd year for the Melrose Inn, operated continuously for that time by members of the Smith family. It's one of the few things on the Cape that I believe has changed very little since 1920, and I hope it doesn't change very much in the future.

MELROSE INN, Harwich Port, Cape Cod, Mass'tts. 02646; 617-432-0171. A village inn on Cape Cod's warm south shore, 12 mi. from Hyannis. American Plan. Breakfast, lunch, dinner served to travelers. Open mid-May to mid-October. Gladys and Philip Smith, Innkeepers.

RALPH WALDO EMERSON, Rockport

"Stop a second," I said, "I think that's the sign."

We were driving through Pigeon Cove on Cape Ann between the stone walls, trees and the Cape Cod saltbox homes that were now many years old. It was a very small sign, and it pointed one block to the right, and sure enough in the midst of all the homes were the rather expansive grounds and imposing pillars of the Ralph Waldo Emerson Inn.

I turned in between the gates and down the gravel walk past a very inviting swimming pool, which I promised to see more of later. I parked and walked back up the driveway and mounted the steps to the broad veranda. There was a most intriguing mixture of people seated enjoying the spectacular view of the ocean, with its offshore rocks and the parade of pleasure and fishing crafts plying the waters in front of the inn.

One of the youngsters collided with me on my way inside and I asked him if the water was cold, it being mid-September. He said, "Oh, no, they have heated water."

Once inside I found a very impressive lobby and living room that was dominated by a sweeping staircase

leading up to the second floor. It was large enough to accommodate some rather large paintings, including Governor Bradford making his first landing. It was heroic in size to say the least. There were other small paintings, and Jan Lindstrom was inspired by one to create the sketch which we've reproduced.

A young man came toward me with a big smile and outstretched hand and said, "Hi, I'm Gary Wemyss. I understand that you have also been staying at the Yankee Clipper with my mother and father." I had heard a lot about Gary from Jim Mellow who had been at the Emerson about ten days earlier and had glowing reports of the good time that he and his wife and children had enjoyed, including a sailboat ride on the bay.

"Oh yes," said Gary, "I remember the Mellows; they're from St. Louis. They were a great deal of fun. By the way, I'm going out on the boat tomorrow, would you care to join me?"

This was the beginning of my stay at the Emerson, and I must say that the stately appearance of this old summer inn somewhat belies its real informality. While everything is well cared for . . . . flowers, hedges, grounds and trees, and the deep-cushioned chairs and sofas are reminiscent of a more formal era, the inn is quite relaxed and compliant. The tone is set by Gary Wemyss:

"I think that people of all interests and ages mix well here," he said. "We find that the easiest thing is not to make any distinction in any way. Everyone seems to enjoy the things that are here . . . the village, the shore, and the nearness to the sea. The feeling of withdrawal of urban pressures and the atmosphere of relaxation brings them all together. They have a wonderful time. They can join in our games or programs, or just sit and rock looking at the ocean."

That's the way it worked for me, too, at the Ralph Waldo Emerson in Pigeon Cove on Cape Ann.

RALPH WALDO EMERSON, 1 Cathedral Ave., Rockport, Mass. 01966; 617-546-6321. A seaside inn, 40 mi. from Boston via Rte.127. Lodgings. Mod. American Plan; European Plan. Breakfast and dinner served daily. Dinner: Jul. 1-Labor Day. Open May 25 — Oct. 15. Gary Wemyss, Innkeeper.

YANKEE CLIPPER, Rockport

The granite boulders loomed all around me, gleaming brightly in the sun. I was glad that I had worn my rubber soled deck shoes. With the aid of some strategically placed rope railings, I picked my way down, almost to the water's edge. On this warm, September morning, it was like a totally different world. There were small tidal pools where I could see bright green moss, and several species of marine life growing. Overhead a few gulls dipped and swooped their way among the changing air currents. I sat with my back against a warm granite boulder, and wished that I had brought my camera with me on this little jaunt.

At dinner the previous evening I had gotten the whole story. Fred and Lydia Wemyss had come here in 1946 on a vacation, when the idea of turning the three homes into an inn occured to them. They have been here ever since.

"These have been wonderful years for us," said Fred, "our son, Gary, and our daughter, Barbara, have both grown up here and Gary has stayed in the innkeeping business with us and is the manager of the Ralph Waldo

Emerson, which you will be visiting while you are here in Pigeon Cove. The most satisfactory part of it all has been the hundreds of people that have become such good friends."

My reverie was broken by the passage of a sailboat in the bay not fifty yards from where I sat sunning myself. I decided to return to reality once again, and went back up the steps to the grassy plateau with the carefully tended flowerbeds, the beautiful terrace, and the grape arbor. Lunch was being served, and everything was shaded by the old New England apple trees.

I strolled underneath the chestnut trees up to the pool where the water was dappled by a brilliant September sun. Experimentally, I stuck my finger in and found it to be gratifyingly warm. "Heated," as Fred explained later.

Around me was a profusion of flowers and bushes, and a beautiful old stone wall. I realized that there must be literally dozens of quiet intimate corners in the inn just like this. In fact, that is a good word to describe the Yankee Clipper — intimate!

Each of the lodging rooms has its own distinct individuality. The dining room, itself, is somewhat elegant, with a beautiful view of both grounds and the sea.

This morning, there was a poem on the blackboard in the dining room beneath the projected weather and temperature:

"A buxom fall foliage tripper
was losing a fight with her zipper.
It's not cause it's old
That the darn thing won't hold,
It's those blueberry cakes at the Clipper."

I suspect such poesy could only come from Fred.

YANKEE CLIPPER, Rockport, Mass. 01966; 617-546-3407. An intimate inn on the sea 45 mi. from Boston via Rte. 127. Lodgings. American Plan: July-Aug; Mod. American Plan: Spring-Fall. Some rooms available on European Plan. Breakfast and dinner served daily. Lunch during July and August. Dining Room open May 15-Oct. 20, inn open April 1st to Nov. 1st. Fred and Lydia Wemyss, Innkeepers.

LONGFELLOW'S WAYSIDE INN, South Sudbury

From my bedroom window I looked through the small forest, and I could plainly see the gleaming spire of the Mary and Martha Chapel in the morning sun. What an interesting contrast to the previous evening, when all of this valley had literally been a fairyland of light. A rain had covered every tree and bush with a thin coating of ice which reflected the outdoor Christmas decorations, and the whole scene was repeated again and again from the crystalline surface of the snow which had acquired a shiny crust. Perhaps the most spectacular sight of all was the ice-encrusted, floodlit Old Mill just up the road.

It was a memorable night. After parking I threw open the wide front door, and there, greeting his guests on New Year's Eve was my good friend, Innkeeper Frank Koppeis.

"Welcome, welcome, good old Berkshire Traveller," he said. "You are thrice welcome indeed."

While I checked in, we chatted about the last time we had met, which was in Kennebunkport, Maine the previous April. Then he took a moment or two from the pressing duties of being a host on New Year's Eve, showed me upstairs to Room 4, and agreed that we would get together later.

The evening had been arranged by my dear friends, Anne Herzog and Karen Brady. A group of us had gathered at the Wayside Inn for a New Year's Eve dinner. Our table was in the Old Kitchen, which tonight rang with the same kind of fun that I am certain characterized the inn under the several innkeepers since 1700. Everything was lit by candlelight, and the low beams and richly panelled walls brought us all closer together.

Antique table

Another thing that brought us all closer together was the food. There were twelve in our party and I think that almost everyone had something different! I ordered duck with orange sauce and when it arrived we were all aghast. It was the largest duck I'd ever been served! It was perfect — the outside was crisp, and the underneath meat was brown and succulent. I topped it off with a piece of Longfellow's Wayside Inn hot deep dish apple pie with real whipped cream.

To help our digestion, after dinner we did what for me was at least my dozenth tour of the famous inn which included, of course, the Longfellow Parlor which inspired the poet's "Tales From A Wayside Inn", and also the Old Tap Room in which there are several large boards used in the original inn. There are also bedrooms on the second floor which have been furnished with period antiques.

Now this morning I would find my way back to the Berkshires, the skies had cleared, and the New Year appeared to be full of promise.

It was, I mused, a most interesting way to see any old year out and any new year in . . . a visit at what Frank Koppeis describes as "the oldest, operating inn in America."

LONGFELLOW'S WAYSIDE INN, Wayside Inn Rd., off Rte. 20, South Sudbury, Mass. 01776; 617-443-8846. A historic landmark inn on Rte. 20 midway between Boston and Worcester. Within short distance of Concord, Lexington and other famous Revolutionary War landmarks. Eastbound on Mass. Pike; Exit at Rte. 495. Northbound:Exit Rte. 20. 8 mi. east on Rte. 20 to inn, 11 mi. west of Rte. 128 on Rte. 20. Lodgings. Lunch and dinner served daily except Christmas. Breakfast to overnight guests. Francis Koppeis, Innkeeper.

LORD JEFFERY INN, Amherst

I had certainly picked a great day to visit the Lord Jeff. It was a bright, sunny, pleasantly cool Saturday afternoon — the day of the Amherst/Williams football game. There are a variety of roads leading from the Berkshires to Amherst, and all of them that day had a number of cars with both Williams and Amherst stickers on the bumper. Actually, there are five colleges within a short distance of one another in this section of Massachusetts, and in many cases the college facilities are combined to provide a better education for everybody concerned.

Just having five colleges in the vicinity would naturally bring a wide variety of guests to the Lord Jeff. Today, there were a number of cars parked around the village green in Amherst, which is ringed by several small shops, including intriguing bookstores and apparel shops that would attract the college-type clientele.

The inn, for the most part, is built of whitewashed red brick with patches of red peeking through. The low ceilinged lobby and parlors are richly panelled and have numerous oil portraits of generals from both sides connected with the French and Indian War. The town, the college, and the inn are named for Lord Jeffery Amherst, who figured prominently in that conflict. The dominant feature of the main living room is the huge fireplace that has, of all things, a window in it. I learned later that the

inn and the fireplace were designed in 1926. I have never seen one similar.

Because I have not mentioned the Lord Jeffery in previous editions, it might be well to point out the fact that Innkeeper Harold Durgin is justifiably proud of the menu offerings.

"We've tried to offer a 'limited number of entrees," he explained, "but what we do, we try to do the very best we can. We take a lot of pains with our turkey and roast beef, and a lot of people tell us that our broiled Boston scrod, which of course is fresh, is excellent. We also have a daily special which we call the 'Innkeeper's Whim'." I looked, and sure enough today's whim was roast native turkey!

Desserts included New England apple pie served with a wedge of sharp cheddar cheese, baked Indian pudding, and peppermint stick ice cream with chocolate sauce. They all sounded yummy.

The Lord Jeffery, like the Williams Inn, serves the interests of a small New England college town. I couldn't help but reflect that there was a wide variety of guests enjoying lunch that particular day, a great many of them tweedy parents accompanied by blue denim clad undergraduates — many with long hair and beards. I guess that it's being run in the tradition of many country inns. Everyone can really feel free to do their own thing.

LORD JEFFERY INN, On the Common, Amherst, Mass. 01002; 413-253-2576. A college town inn in western Massachusetts. Open year 'round. Lodgings. Breakfast, lunch, dinner served every day in the year to travelers. xc ski. Harold and Janice Durgin, Innkeepers.

THE NIGHT THE REVOLUTION BEGAN

In 1773, the British imposed a tax upon all tea imported to the colonies, a tax many of the citizens of Massachusetts were determined not to pay. In late November of that year, three tea ships appeared in Boston Harbor, and British warships hovered nearby to protect them. Indignant citizens met at Old South Meeting House on December 16, determined to prevent the tea from being landed. Thus it was the day of "The Night the Revolution Began." The following quotes are from the book of that name by Wesley S. Griswold, published in 1972 by the Stephen Greene Press of Brattleboro, Vermont, and reprinted here with the kind permission of the publisher. The first quotation is from the speech by Josiah Quincy, a true patriot but one who that day was pleading moderation:

"It is not, Mr. Moderator, the spirit that vapors without these walls that must stand us in stead. The exertions of this day will call forth the events which will make a very different spirit necessary for our salvation. Whoever supposes that shouts and hosannas will terminate the trials of the day entertains a childish fancy. We must be grossly ignorant of the importance and value of the prize for which we contend; we must be equally ignorant of the power of those who have combined against us; we must be blind to that malice, inveteracy, and insatiable revenge which actuates our enemies, public and private, abroad and in our bosom, to hope that we shall end this controversy without the sharpest—the sharpest—conflicts; to flatter ourselves that popular resolves, popular harangues, popular acclamations, and popular vapor will vanquish our foes.

'Let us consider the issue. Let us look to the end. Let us weigh and consider before we ad-

vance to those measures which must bring on the most trying and terriffic struggle this country ever saw."

The Boston Gazette, on December 20, reported:

"But, BEHOLD, what followed! A number of brave & resolute men, determined to do all in their power to save their country from the ruin which their enemies had plotted, in less than four hours emptied every chest of tea on board the three ships commanded by the captains Hall, Bruce and Coffin, amounting to 324 chests, into the sea! Without the least damage done to the ships or any other property."

And the mate of one of the ships, the Dartmouth, recorded:

"Between six and seven o'clock this evening came down to the wharf a body of about one thousand people. Among them were a number dressed and whopping like Indians. They came on board the ship, and after warning myself and the Custom-House officer to get out of the way, they unlaid the hatches and went down the hold, where was eighty whole and thirty-four half chests of Tea, which they hoisted upon deck, and cut the chests to pieces, and hove the Tea all overboard, where it was damaged and lost."

But it remained for an anonymous New Hampshire poet, three years later, to best sum up the results of the Boston Tea Party:

"What discontents, what dire events,
From trifling things proceed?
A little Tea, thrown in the sea,
Has thousands caused to bleed."

YANKEE PEDLAR, Holyoke

On each visit to the Yankee Pedlar it seems that Gene Tamburi has had some kind of expansion program in progress. This time it was the recent completion of the Opera House which is now the showpiece of the inn. It is the replica of an old Victorian theatre and was created with old materials gathered during the past ten years. The first thing that caught my eye was the glittering crystal chandelier which Innkeeper Bess Stathis told me came from the Metropolitan Opera House in New York. The heroic-size paintings, like many of the decorations in the other parts of the inn, came from Kenilworth Castle, a beautiful old estate which was a replica of an English castle.

To me, one of the most impressive things about this inn is the number of dining rooms and the number of people that can be served at one time. Yet, because the seven dining rooms are all rather small and individual, I always have the feeling of intimacy. There are dining rooms with stone floors and barn siding; still another strikes a predominantly masculine note with exposed beams and leather covered chairs and banquettes. There is also the Old Oyster Bar which was built from old oak panelling and decorated with Tiffany lamps, replicas of old gaslights and deep red carpeting. Oysters, clams, shrimp and hearty sandwiches are on the Bill of Fare.

Scattered throughout the inn are dozens of artifacts and objets d'art from the 19th century. There is much old pewter, silverware and glassware. Old prints are to be found on all walls, and the newest acquisition is a handsome old ice box with brass hardware.

The menu also provides a traveler with a most enticing introduction to New England. There is seafood from the cold, northeast waters, as well as beef, fowl and other hearty country fare.

Because Holyoke is just a few minutes driving distance from such excellent colleges and preparatory schools as Mt. Holyoke, Smith, Amherst, University of Massachusetts and New Hampshire, there is quite apt to be a sprinkling of students or prospective students and parents who use the inn as a sort of command post in search for higher education.

During dinner that evening, our waiter, Albert, joined the other waiters and waitresses to sing "Happy Birthday" to a guest at an adjoining table. The singing was a little off key but nevertheless sincere! However, pictorially it was a very happy sight to see the girls in their gingham dresses and the boys in their green butcher-boy uniforms gathered around the candlelit table singing with such evident gusto.

As I made my way up the narrow stairway to a very cozy bedroom, it occurred to me that Gene and Kate Tamburi have preserved and restored some of the best of old New England in this inn located in the beautiful Pioneer Valley of western Massachusetts.

YANKEE PEDLAR INN, Holyoke, Mass'tts. 01040; 413-532-9494. A village inn a few minutes from the Mass. Tpke. (east-west) and I-91 (north-south), Exit 202. Near Old Storrowtown, a reproduction of a colonial western Mass'tts. village, and the Eastern States Exposition Grounds. Lodgings. (Cont. Breakfast to house guests only). Lunch and dinner served every day except Christmas. Oyster Bar open from 11a.m. to 12:30a.m. daily. Opens 5p.m. Sat. and Sun. Alpine and xc ski. Bess Stathis, Innkeeper.

Williamstown is a small community of obvious tradition and a great deal of ambiance. It is, in fact, as New England a college town as one will find, and the Williams Inn is totally in keeping with it.

In many respects, Williamstown is the kind of college town you always wanted to find but never thought you would. It is located in the upper northwest corner of the Berkshires, and from almost any direction the roads leading into town are very attractive and the views are gratifying to spectacular.

I always make it a point to stop in and see Ralph Renzi of the College Bookstore and express my envy of a very fine selection of books. Then, it's fun to stop and get two warm rolls at the bakery, next door. The residential streets are broad with large elms, oaks and pines and from most anywhere in town you can see the surrounding mountain ranges.

THE WILLIAMS INN, Williamstown

Williamstown doorway

Innkeeper John Treadway was becoming a bit philosophic. "Well, the best laid plans of mice and men . . . however, all we have done is to postpone the new Williams Inn for just one more year. Actually, the zoning had to be changed before the permit to build could be issued," he explained. "We expected to be building at this time, but now the anticipated occupancy date is April 1, 1974." The new location is well-suited.

In a sense, this reprieve of one year for what might be called the "changing of the guards" will give all of the Williams' Alumni another year in which to wander about in what is no doubt their favorite country inn. They might even sit at the big, battered table that is covered with initials and reminisce, perhaps finding a familiar pair. John assured me that this, among other things, would also be moved to the new inn upon completion.

"Among the things we also hope to move are the bird feeders and probably some of the surrounding bushes and shrubs," he pointed out. The present bird feeding stations that are plainly visible from the picture windows are extremely well-known, and I am sure that many varieties of New England birds, both winter and summer can be observed. John is a very enthusiastic "birder" and can with a great show of modesty, discuss birds and their habits at great length.

And so, this is positively the last issue of "Country Inns and Back Roads" which will deal with the old Williams Inn which was started in 1912 by John Treadway's father, L.G. Treadway. It was, in fact, the beginning of the whole Treadway Inn idea.

John went on to say, "Dad is 89 this year and we're still running the inn with a great many of his basic ideas. Good regional food, lots of it, and personalized hospitality. There is really no reason to change it."

I'm sure that many of the men (and now women) of Williams will echo that most exuberantly!

WILLIAMS INN, Williamstown, Mass'tts. 01267; 413-458-5711. A secluded village inn on the campus of Williams College. Lodgings. Breakfast, lunch, dinner served daily. 24 college tennis courts adjacent to inn. Alpine and xc ski. John Treadway, Innkeeper.

MORGAN HOUSE, Lee

I leaned over for a closer look. There it was. Unmistakable: U.S. Grant; Sunday, November 27, 1883.

We were looking at an old register sheet from the Morgan House, for many years a Berkshire stage stop. There were many other great and near-greats listed. Some of the interesting signatures were done in elaborate scrolls and old penmanship by members of traveling theatrical groups. Evidently, they saw an opportunity for some free advertising. Dee and Lou Schroeter told me about a lady who, when looking over the list, suddenly exclaimed: "There's Grandfather!"

These old sheets now paper the lobby wall of this village inn. Each time I visit, I find a new and unusual registrant.

Lee is a very bustling town near the western end of the Massachusetts Turnpike. On that particular warm

Lee village green

Tuesday the guests seemed to be pretty divided among people who were visiting and business people from the local area who were enjoying a brief respite from the day's labors. Many of them were old friends of mine, who stopped for a word or two of greeting before continuing.

I followed Lou through the dinning room with the low ceiling and warm panelling, into the spotless kitchen where the evening meal was in its initial stages. Freshly baked pies were out on the big table, small loaves of bread were warm and aromatic. Waitresses were bustling in and out of the dining room. One of them said: "So you're the Berkshire Traveller. With all that eating, I never expected to see someone so slim!"

I looked at the evening menu with roast lamb, baked stuffed shrimp, London broil and all those creamy, dreamy pies and wondered how much longer she'd be able to say that.

MORGAN HOUSE, Main St., Lee, Mass. 01238; 413-243-0181. A village inn in the Berkshires just a few miles from Tanglewood and Jacob's Pillow. A few unassuming lodging rooms available. Lunch and dinner served daily except Mondays and Labor Day. Alpine and xc ski. Lou and Dee Schroeter, Innkeepers.

THE RED LION INN, Stockbridge

"We arbitrarily chose the date because I don't believe that anyone really knows when The Red Lion Inn first opened." Jane Fitzpatrick and I were seated in one of the side parlors of The Red Lion discussing the bicentennial celebration of the Inn which is planned for the second Thursday in June. It seemed rather appropriate to be talking in this particular room because there were rockers, corner cupboards, tables and chests which had been collected by various owners and innkeepers over the years.

"We want to do something very simple," she said, "but at the same time recognize that the Inn was established at least 200 years ago. In 1773, it was a three story building on this very site, with 8 bedrooms and a bath on the third floor.

"We are planning to have a little ceremony in the morning, hoping the Governor, prominent persons, and even the President and Mrs. Nixon will join us. In the afternoon, there will be an Open House for all the people in the community. Should be an interesting day!"

We went into the main living room of the Inn where a low fire burned in the fireplace and where the antique desks and highboys were an interesting contrast to the community bulletin board crammed full with upcoming area events. Even as we sat talking about the bicentennial, several of the Stockbridge townspeople passed through, busily pursuing some business in the Inn.

Four new visitors to Stockbridge came through the front door of the inn and immediately stopped to admire the collection of pitchers and plates adorning the shelves above the doorways and arches. "Almost everyone comments on them," remarked Jane, "and so many people ask about our old Grandfather's clocks."

The Red Lion is a great many things to a great many people. For the town of Stockbridge, it is a meeting place and shared community experience. Almost everything of

public importance takes place here. Some of the best arguments after the Town Meetings adjourn to Widow Bingham's Tavern, one of the inn's dining rooms.

To the out-of-town guest, the inn and the village itself combine to create a brief visit to an almost idealized New England experience.

For the summer visitor, the many activities include Tanglewood Music Festival, The Berkshire Playhouse, The Corner House, where Norman Rockwell's original paintings are exhibited, and Jacob's Pillow.

In winter, the Inn becomes a snug retreat for quiet times away from the city, with alpine and cross-country skiing in the vicinity, and ice skating.

THE RED LION INN, Stockbridge, Massachusetts, 01262; (413) 298-5545. An historic village inn on Rte. 7 in the Berkshires. Adjacent to Tanglewood, Berkshire Theatre, Jacob's Pillow and major ski areas. Lodgings. Breakfast, lunch, dinner served daily. Jack and Jane Fitzpatrick, Innkeepers.

STAGECOACH HILL, Sheffield

I like to arrive at Stagecoach Hill just at dusk. Carefully tended stone walls in this rolling countryside are now vague shapes; in the distance a light on the magnificent sign and the old red brick building welcomes me.

The main entrance is through some ponderous Victorian doors, up a short flight of stairs to a lounge area which is dimly lit by flickering candles in red jars. In winter additional light is provided by fires on two raised hearths.

More candles light the dining rooms which look very inviting with their red tablecloths, white napkins and gleaming silverware. The walls have sporting and hunting prints, and a new addition is a large poster recently acquired by Scotty which shows horsemen returning from an English hunt.

Scotty and I had a lot to talk about. He was most enthusiastic about the way things were going. "We've been making new friends all the time," he said, "and people seem to like our food. We have a separate menu for Saturday which includes roast beef, barbecue spareribs, duckling in orange sauce, and chicken livers wrapped in bacon and served with rice.

"I think that our most popular main dishes are the plank sirloin steak, the steak and mushroom pie, and the Alderman's Carpetbag which is a steak with six oysters cooked inside it."

An English trifle arrived at the table simultaneous with our discussion about desserts. "Weel, I think that's the favorite," he said, his burr getting a little stronger. "But the Stilton cheese, Bavarian cream pie and chocolate eclairs are good also. We have a young man who does the pastry cooking who studied in Vienna.

"Ye know, we're just a wee inn," he said. "We've

Mountain brook

only got ten rooms, and some of them are going to be redecorated very shortly. However, there are lots of people who seem to find our location off the beaten track, just right for a bit of quiet rest. The brook runs right behind our chalets with a most musical sound, and there are lots of birds in the forest."

Speaking of birds, I was awestruck, to say the least, by the imposing sight of three peacocks who have free reign of all the grounds. Scotty said that he expected to have several more in just a few weeks. "The guests find them fascinating," he said. At this point one of the males ruffled up his feathers into that amazing arrangement that suggested he was posing for NBC.

Scotty's only comment was — " 'Tis the mating season, ye know!"

STAGECOACH HILL INN, Under Mountain Rd., Sheffield, Mass'tts. 01257; 413-229-8585. A British inn with Scottish overtones in the Berkshires, located on Rte. 41, mid-way between Salisbury and Great Barrington. Near southern Berkshire chairlift areas and summertime attractions. Lodgings. Dinner nightly and all day Sunday. Closed Christmas Eve and Christmas Day. Scotty Burns and Wilbur Wheeler, Innkeepers.

Rhode Island

We ascertained that there is a great deal more to experience in Rhode Island than we'd ever imagined. The smallest state in the Union has much history, recreation, excellent back roads and fine beaches. For some years we've stayed at a village inn near the south shore at Wakefield.

LARCHWOOD INN, Wakefield

Frank Browning looked up from the open grill on the patio with a twinkle in his eye. "This," he said, "is yours," indicating with a long-pronged fork one of the steaks on the real charcoal fire.

The lady standing next to me asked, "Which one is mine?" Frank said, "The one up in the corner is yours, you said you wanted medium, didn't you?"

I was at the Larchwood Inn during Memorial Day weekend, and the spring flowers and flowering fruit trees were in their most delightful profusion. The red maples and pine trees were shimmering in the afternoon sun. There were both steaks and lobsters being done on the grill, and although there was no hint of rain in the air, the blue and white striped cover overhead would certainly protect us.

While we were watching Francis being happy in his work, I discovered this lady was part of a family of four that had sailed up the Connecticut and Rhode Island coast from Greenwich, Connecticut and were enjoying a treat of a dinner ashore. "We just love this section of Rhode Island. The countryside is so pretty and there is a great deal of history to poke into."

The Larchwood, itself, reflects these engaging features of Southern Rhode Island. Actually, it is a large

Narragansett trawler

mansion with very comfortable lodging rooms and food that reflects the off-shore fishing, as well as the hearty farm products.

The interior has many Scottish touches, including quotations from Robert Burns and Sir Walter Scott, and photographs and prints of Scottish historical and literary figures. One of the dining rooms has wall paintings showing farm and seascapes of Southern Rhode Island.

Rhode Island is a state of stone walls. They come in various heights, thicknesses and conditions of repair. The back roads which are most numerous for a state that is reputedly small often come upon some interesting historical sites, as well as beautiful homes. There is much for the seeing and doing, I discovered, within a short distance of the Larchwood.

The steak was done to perfection. The boating family invited me to sail across the bay to Martha's Vineyard the next day with them. It sounded like a great idea. I could hardly wait to see Arthur Young's expression when he looked out of his window at the Harborside Inn and sees me tying up a 21-foot sailboat at the dock in Edgartown!

LARCHWOOD INN, 176 Main St., Wakefield, R.I. 02879; 401-783-5454. A village inn just 3 mi. from the famous southern R.I. beaches. Lodgings. Breakfast, lunch, dinner served daily. Francis Browning, Innkeeper.

Connecticut

Most people want to get out of the city to the Connecticut hinerland in a big hurry, and as a result some of the more interesting roads are passed up in favor of the super highways. One should try some of the unmarked roads in Fairfield County. Certainly the Merritt Parkway and the Connecticut Turnpike do very nicely as far as Westport, but there, we suggest picking out some of the roads that lead north through Wilton an on up through Ridgefield and past Danbury.

One of the prettiest roads in Connecticut is that section of Route 7 which starts in Kent and goes through Cornwall Bridge, West Cornwall and Falls Village into northwest Connecticut where there are several country inns. This road runs right next to the plunging Housatonic River.

The new Connecticut country inn in this edition is at Litchfield, which is located on Route 25 between Torrington and Waterbury.

HOMESTEAD INN, Greenwich

I remember the letter well. In fact, I may have mentioned it before. It was the kind of letter we love to receive and convinces us that we're on the right track!

"My husband and I," she said in part, "have been coming to New York for years. Last winter we ran across the book in which you spoke of how convenient the Homestead Inn in Greenwich was to the city. We took a chance and made reservations, and it was beautiful.

"Clean and quiet rooms, and I liked the Colonial furniture. My husband was able to arrange his appointments in the city by telephone from our room and we took the mid-morning, uncrowded train to Grand Central. It took just 45 minutes.

"I did some shopping, he did his business, we met for a matinee, and had dinner at the Algonquin. Then, back to Greenwich for a heavenly, peaceful sleep.

"The second day we came back from town in mid-afternoon and had a very nice dinner at the Homestead. Mr. Estes, himself, entertained at the organ after dinner, and we met some very nice people from Chicago. We also made reservations for our trip in January."

In my many visits to the Homestead I found that while many people from out-of-town enjoy staying there, there are also a considerable number of city mice who enjoy getting out into the country. This may well be the closest country inn to New York, at least one with lodgings available. Both Cal and Vincent are from the city, and while you might be able to take the boy out of the city, you can't take all of the city out of the boy; so naturally there are some areas such as the continental selections on the menu that indicate an urban sophistication. However, I was very surprised to see how many real country items were included. In fact, when I closed my eyes while eating the apple pie I could have sworn I was at the Rabbit Hill Inn in Lower Waterford, Vermont.

HOMESTEAD INN, 420 Field Point Rd., Greenwich, Conn. 06830; 203-869-7500. A sophisticated country inn on an old estate in the residential section of Greenwich. Exit 3, Conn. Thwy. Lodgings. Lunch and dinner served to travelers every day. Lunch not served Saturday. Cal Estes and Vincent Morino, Innkeepers.

KILRAVOCK INN, Litchfield

I swung my car around the turns, over the brook, past the broad fields and a very neat stone wall. On my left there was a sign that said: "Kilravock, A Country Inn." I turned in between the stone gates and pulled up to what was to all intents a Scottish Manor House. There were Tudor half-timbers and many, many windows with smaller English-type panes. When I pushed the great wooden door open, there at the far end of the main hall was a fire burning in a recessed fireplace.

This was Kilravock. It may take quite a few editions to tell its whole story, but its beginning is worth noting now.

Phil and Lis Hoyt had gotten in touch with me during the Fall of 1971 and wanted to talk about buying a country inn. I invited them to lunch at the Red Lion Inn and found them to be an attractive, vibrant couple. We also had dinner that night at the Morgan House in Lee. The upshot of it was, was that they wanted to leave Greenwich, Connecticut and the rat race in and out of New York to Phil's brokerage business. They thought a country inn was the answer. Frankly, I tried to talk them out of it.

I explained all the pitfalls, and referred them to Connie and Ray Bergendoff in Lyme, New Hampshire for whom we had found a country inn a few years ago. Apparently it was to no avail, as about two weeks later they called on the phone and said they had found a beautiful place in the Litchfield hills and would I come and visit them after they had had a chance to get adjusted. This was that visit.

The Kilravock (pronounced Kil-rook) is doing well, thank you. Lis has easily channeled her enthusiasm and knowledge of gourmet cooking into the kitchen and dining room. Phil has put many innovations and ingenuity into the "front of the house."

I asked the Hoyts what was the most satisfactory aspect of innkeeping. Here are some of the comments they had: "The greatest satisfaction is in being able to serve people." "We try to give people what they don't get at home — being waited on, smiles, breakfast in bed if they like, though they must advise us the night before." "I like to prepare interesting first courses–escarole soup as an example. Main courses include frogs legs and shrimp provencale–veal scallopini–Danish roast duck–homemade pasta dishes are all very special.

The rooms, the well-kept grounds, the swimming pool and tennis courts all combine to make what one of the guests described as a "picture book inn." In winter the inn's surroundings are most adaptable to cross-country skiing.

Last Fall, I received a telephone call from a young man who wanted to be married at a country inn. I gave him several suggestions, and he chose Kilravock. He later called to tell me everything was perfect. It may start a trend!

KILRAVOCK INN, Brush Hill Rd., Litchfield, Conn. 06759; 203-567-8100. A secluded country resort inn ½ mi. off Rte. 25, 2 mi. west of the historic village of Litchfield. Lodgings. European Plan. Meals served to travelers daily except Wed. noon and evening and Sun. evening. Closed Christmas Day. Open all year. Phil and Lis Hoyt, Innkeepers.

WHITE HART INN, Salisbury

On the telephone, John Harney was quasi-terse: "Berkshire Traveller, you've got to come down here and see this Gingerbread Village. Did you know that it was featured in the December issue of Woman's Day?"

In the face of such earth-shaking news, there was aught that I could do but make an early appearance and have dinner with the benign, self-styled hotelier of the White Hart.

One of my favorite approaches to Lakeville and Salisbury is the road from Sharon. Leaving Sharon village, the road has a definite ascent and crests the hill with a beautiful white house on the right side of the road that has very impressive porches and pillars. I have often wondered about the people who live there. The view to the southwest includes the beautiful rolling hills and a lake. The road then drops down to pass Hotchkiss School, just outside of Lakeville, and turns east among the Colo-

Gingerbread village

nial houses of both Lakeville and Salisbury, eventually coming to the village green and the White Hart Inn.

John Harney, like other innkeepers of my acquaintance, has almost become a legend in his own time. He is a two times, unsuccessful candidate for state office, but says he hasn't lost heart yet. He has a remarkable memory for names and details, and an unflagging sense of good humor. I caught him cheating at checkers in 1967 and reported it to my readers at that time. Perhaps, in spite of him, the White Hart is a notable country inn!

Come to think of it, it has a lot going for it. It first opened about 100 years ago, and has an ideal setting in a Currier and Ives northwest Connecticut town. The dining room and living rooms are comfortable and homelike, and the White Hart Country Store, right off the lobby, attracts a constant parade of curious people.

It turned out that he was serious about my seeing the Gingerbread Village, and I'm glad that I did. It is the work of Olive DuBois of Salisbury, who is on the staff of the inn, and is laid out on two huge tables. It consists of many country village buildings. They include a carrousel, a country store, a schoolhouse and a church. I studied them for a long time and kept seeing new things happening, including a wedding taking place in the church. Olive told me that she starts working on it early in November and has been creating it for some years. It is really a work of art and a labor of love.

I was amazed to discover that except for the frames, the whole village is edible. When I reached over to break off a piece of the gingerbread roof, John Harney's hand, with the deft practice that has made him the fastest gun in town, caught my wrist in a vice of iron, and through taut lips, and fastening me with his frosty stare, said:

"The man who touches that gingerbread has to answer to me."

Sometimes he's really too much.

WHITE HART INN, Salisbury, Conn. 06068; 203-435-2511. A village inn at the Jct. of US 44 & 41. 55 mi. West of Hartford. Lodgings. Lunch and dinner served daily. Alpine, xc and ski-jumping. John Harney, Innkeeper.

MOUNTAIN VIEW INN, Norfolk

One of the things I like to eat is duck. I've had duck all over the United States. I've even had duck at Firpo's Restaurant in Calcutta, India, but that's another story! It may just be that I have found the quintessence of duck. Oddly enough, it was at Mountain View Inn in Norfolk, Connecticut just about forty-five minutes away from my home in the Berkshires.

In my mind's eye, I can see the inn the last time I paid them a visit during the Christmas holidays. My first impression was one of real hominess; there was a Christmas tree decorated in the old fashioned way, the way I used to decorate it when I was a child. Cards from dozens of friends and patrons of the inn festooned the mantle of the fireplace. In a tiny lobby there was a small aquarium bubbling away in the corner, and there was also Karl Jokinen's growing collection of clocks.

Yale mansion in Norfolk

In one of the parlors there were several tables laden with jellies, jams, cookies, fresh bread (from Karl's oven), and other countrified delicacies. In some ways this New England bucolia somewhat belies the extreme sophistication of the Mountain View menu. The evening that I was there, Karl and Joan and I had an opportunity to reminisce about Karl's early days as an apprentice in the Ritz-Carlton and Somerset Club in Boston.

"Oh yes, I started at the bottom, and every time I would make a move the new chef would tell me that I didn't really know anything and I'd have to start in all over again." Karl laughs as he thinks about it now. "Well, this place is a realization of a dream for us. It's just the kind of community for which we were looking, and we have enough lodging rooms to accommodate a comfortable number of people. It is a lovely area for raising children, and it is a real family operation, with Joan's mother and father as well."

The menu reflects Karl's twenty-five years of experience, and includes frogs legs, real Smithfield ham, loin of pork, stuffed shrimp, Boston scrod, and the duck. Ah the duck. . . .it is crisp on the outside, delightfully warm and tender on the inside, with a delicious helping of stuffing underneath, and a sauce that defies my poor description. Also on the plate, beautifully arranged, were baked apples stuffed with mincemeat. The crowning touch came when Joan poured a little cointreau over it, applied a match, and for an instant or two there was a bright blue flame.

They didn't do that in Calcutta.

MOUNTAIN VIEW INN, Norfolk, Conn. 06058; 203-542-5595. A village inn on Rtes. 44 & 272, 40 mi. west of Hartford in the picturesque Litchfield Hills. Lodgings. Breakfast, lunch and dinner served daily except Monday. George and Helen Linonis. Alpine and xc ski. Karl Jokinen, Chef/Innkeeper.

BOULDERS INN, New Preston

At the Boulders they are the third and fourth generations carrying on the innkeeping tradition, making new friends by the score each year. Grandfather bought the 250 acres of shores, fields, and woodlands, and gained fame for his generous hospitality about 80 years ago. Now, the Boulders is still a family affair with Dick and Jane Lowe and their two sons making it a real way of life.

Here is an excerpt from a letter I received from them during mid-winter:

Swimming in Lake Waramaug

"Our year has been a good one. As usual, we have had a nucleus of 'regulars' plus the always welcome new faces, including a number who have come from reading about us in 'Country Inns and Back Roads.' Happily, they have a good idea from the book about what we are like and settle right down in. They fit right in with our other guests in our more or less casual atmosphere, and we enjoy having them. The largest number of those travelling with the book are young couples, both with and without children. They come from all over the country.

"Speaking of your readers, we found that they are particularly appreciative of the unspoiled country and like the outdoors. They are intelligent and self-sufficient in entertaining themselves. A lot of them read the many books we have here.

"During the past year we continued to re-model our shorefront and kitchen. We do not plan to increase our capacity, as our present size permits personal hospitality and allows us to spend as much time as possible with our guests.

"Dick continues to be active as chairman of the zoning commission and former chairman of the Lake Waramaug Authority. We stay busy and happy year 'round in our little Connecticut hideaway."

I guess that tells the story on the Boulders. The Lowes are nice people who run a very trim inn on a lake in a farm setting. Incidentally, the cross-country skiing on the hill in back among the woods is first-rate.

I'm sure Grandfather would heartily approve.

BOULDERS INN, Lake Waramaug, New Preston, Conn. 06777; 203-868-7918. A year 'round resort-inn on Conn. Rte. 45, 1½ mi. north of New Preston, 20 mi. from Danbury. American and Mod. American Plans, mid-June to mid-September; European Plan all year. Breakfast, lunch, dinner served to travelers mid-June to mid-September. Dinners not served Monday during summer. Bed and breakfast all year, other meals as above. Closed Thanksgiving and Christmas. Alpine and xc ski. Dick and Jane Lowe, Innkeepers.

COUNTRY SQUIRE, Killingworth

I remember my first time at the Country Squire. Louis had restrained himself from talking about it because he thought my first look should be untrammeled by bias.

As soon as I saw it — I was forever trammeled by bias.

This is a little gem of a country inn in a devotedly maintained setting of rich green grass, bushes, and trees in varying stages of bloom. There are even lawn bowling and croquet.

The white narrow-clapboard house was built around 1794 by one, Squire Evarts. It's been augmented over the years by several connecting out-buildings, including a jaunty buggy shed, which is a warm weather dining area.

The interior, with low ceiling, chair rails, 18th century fireplaces, and handsome, wide floor boards has been further enhanced with a prodigious collection of antiques and artifacts ranging from the Colonial period through the 19th century.

To enter, we picked our way through the terrace with many people enjoying the late afternoon breeze. Inside, the first thing I saw was a three-sided counter with an overhead wicket. Right next to that was a little secret rendezvous which is called the "Squire's Corner."

Each successive room held more delightful surprises. The main dining room was a story and a half high with many pitchers, plates, and wooden decoys decorating its beams.

The next room was called the "Longfellow Room" in honor of the fact that the poet has written a piece called "The Birds of Killingworth." This looks out over the lawn and gardens and has a very lighthearted atmosphere.

Louis and Dottie Matsikas have carefully recreated a very few lodging rooms in keeping the basic atmosphere of the inn. However, as in the case with all of these country inns, it is best to telephone ahead for reservations in order to avoid disappointment.

Later, I wandered out to the shops in the red barn. Dottie found me there and said that it was dinner time. From the offerings on the menu, I knew that it was going to be a great evening.

COUNTRY SQUIRE, P.O. Box 8, Deep River, Conn. 06417; 203-669-5764. A country inn on Rte. 80, 5 mi. from Exit 63 Conn. Tpke. Lodgings. Lunch and dinner served every day except Monday noon, and Christmas Day. Louis and Dottie Matsikas, Innkeepers.

Mid Atlantic

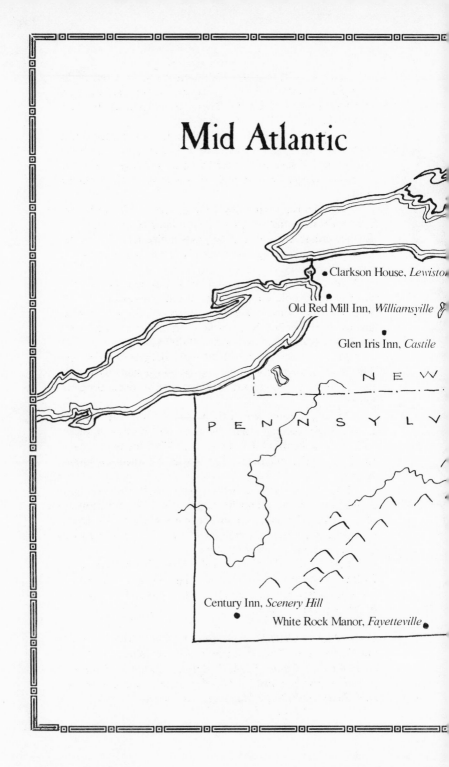

Clarkson House, *Lewiston*

Old Red Mill Inn, *Williamsville*

Glen Iris Inn, *Castile*

N E W

P E N N S Y L V

Century Inn, *Scenery Hill*

White Rock Manor, *Fayetteville*

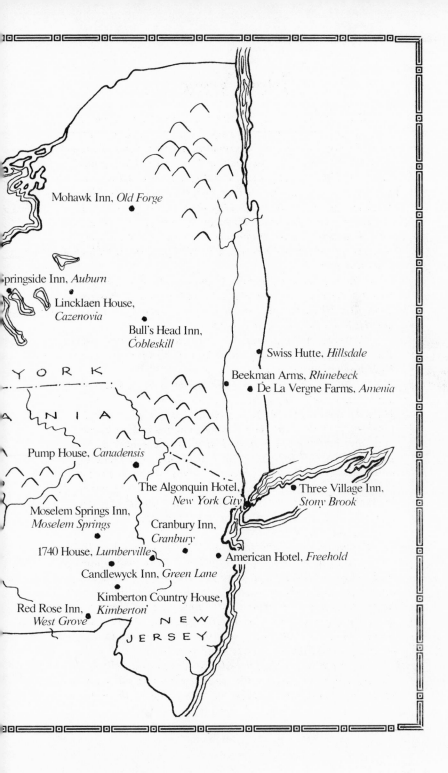

Mohawk Inn, *Old Forge*

Springside Inn, *Auburn*

Lincklaen House,
Cazenovia

Bull's Head Inn,
Cobleskill

Swiss Hutte, *Hillsdale*

Beekman Arms, *Rhinebeck*
De La Vergne Farms, *Amenia*

Y O R K

A N I A

Pump House, *Canadensis*

The Algonquin Hotel,
New York City

Three Village Inn,
Stony Brook

Moselem Springs Inn,
Moselem Springs

Cranbury Inn,
Cranbury

1740 House, *Lumberville*

American Hotel, *Freehold*

Candlewyck Inn, *Green Lane*

Kimberton Country House,
Kimberton

Red Rose Inn,
West Grove

N E W
J E R S E Y

New York

Being a country boy I can't really say I am much of an authority on traveling in New York City, but I've always found that the least aggravating east-west streets are principle two-way arteries such as 14th, 23rd, 34th, 42nd, 57th, or 72nd. In any case, it takes patience. However, once on either the East River Drive or the West Side Highway going north (preferably at a non-traffic time) I go up the Sawmill River Parkway to the Taconic Parkway. This is one of the original New York State Parkways and because it does not permit trucks or trailers, is still a beautiful experience.

The Taconic goes to East Chatham where it links up with the New York State Thruway and the Massachusetts Turnpike. However, country inns in Rhinebeck, Amenia and Hillsdale are quite accessible.

Chatham is on a latitude with the Berkshires, and Route 22 or Route 7 may be followed north to further New England country inns.

Assuming, however, we are going west into New York State, let's cross the river between Catskill and Hudson and take the back roads through places like Clarksville, Berne and Gallupville. They are all on the map, and half the fun is to find them. The objective is to stop at Cobleskill for either lunch or dinner and proceed north picking up Route 20 at Sharon. Now the great panorama of New York is stretched out to the west. The road leads through Sangerville and Morrisville with a stop off at Cazenovia, then on to Auburn perhaps for overnight at the country inn.

Before leaving Auburn, I find Castile on the map. It is in a patch of green southwest of Rochester in the middle of Letchworth State Park. Short of playing tag with all the Finger Lakes, the best way to Castile is to continue on Route 20 to 20A just west of Canandaguia. At Geneseo there are the first signs for Letchworth State Park. The ride through the park to the southwest corner next to the gorge of the Genesee River is most pleasant.

We're really headed for Buffalo and Niagara Falls on this particular trip, and there are really nothing but back roads to the outskirts, where the best thing to do is to follow the interstates and limited access highways to Lewiston, and a new inn.

It will be necessary to double back a bit mentally, to find the road to another one of our new country inns located in Old Forge. There is only one road—Route 28. It is right in the middle of the Adirondacks, and while there are some back roads in that section of the country I would suggest waiting until you've arrived before heading into the green forest. You could really get lost!

THE ALGONQUIN, New York City

The principle satisfaction out of writing this book is to hear from people each year who have had happy experiences at the inns mentioned therein. This is particularly true of the Hotel Algonquin in New York City.

To begin with, we could hardly term New York City "the country." But a few years ago I found myself in the same predicament quite frequently — many of my correspondents, anxious to use this book as a reference (for which we are most flattered), were planning to fly to New York from points literally all over the globe and then proceed in three of the four directions going from inn to inn. The question was: Where could one stay in New York? Frankly, that baffled me for quite awhile until Andy Anspach, the innkeeper at the Algonquin Hotel, suggested that I come to New York and see whether or not I agreed with him that the Algonquin had "all the endearing qualities of a fine country inn."

I did, and it does. So, I included it.

Now, please allow me to share with you the enthusiasm of a young couple from Washington, D.C. who wrote recently: "We are so pleased with the Algonquin that we must share our thoughts with you. The staff is superior in

United Nations building

all ways and at all times. Our six weeks in New York were a joy, due in part to the Algonquin, which we refer to as an oasis in the big city."

The Algonquin really started making its own history in the 1920's and '30s when it was the meeting place for a group of certain New York literati who found the environment commensurate with their own unique high spirits. It was at that time that the famous Round Table (still the third on the right in the Oak Room) came into being, and young writers like Mark Connolly, Edna Ferber, Dorothy Parker, Robert Benchley, and New Yorker editor, Harold Ross, met for lunch and continued their elaborate admiration for each other.

This history goes on every day because many rather glamorous guests from the world of entertainment, arts and government regard this rather conservative atmosphere of the hotel as their escape from the public eye.

Over the years the decor in the Oak Room and the Edwardian lobby has been touched-up a bit, but on the whole it remains much the same as it has for the past fifty years. This holds true in the lodging rooms where there is a dignity in the old-fashioned furniture, the lighting fixtures, and the very deep bath tubs. I have also found there is a feeling of pride in the old-fashioned concept of room service at the Algonquin, and it is still one of my greatest treats to order breakfast while there and have it arrive in my room in almost jig time along with the morning paper.

Realizing that many of our readers are visiting New York for the first time, I'm happy to know that starting with the doorman right through to the bellmen, room clerks, elevator operators, waiters, and Andy Anspach himself, the out-of-town guest is regarded as another fellow human being by the Algonquin staff, instead of just a room number or a potential tip.

New York, like many other large cities, can be something of a letdown, and I think that the Algonquin is more exciting than the city itself.

ALGONQUIN HOTEL, 59 W. 44th St., New York, N.Y. 10036; 212-687-4400. A quiet, conservative country inn in the heart of Manhattan. Convenient to business, theatres, and shopping. Lodgings. Breakfast, lunch, dinner, supper served every day. Andrew Anspach, Innkeeper.

BEEKMAN ARMS, Rhinebeck

"I've heard lots of explanations for the name 'Rynbeck'," said Chuck LaForge, as we sat down for dinner in the low-ceilinged tap room of America's oldest inn, "but recently I learned that on a ship coming to this country with Peter Stuyvesant came a German, William Beckman who originally came from the Rine Valley. His son received a grant for land here from Queen Anne

Seventeenth century sailing ship

of England in 1703, and he named the property Rhinebeck. I guess to move from the word 'Beck' to 'Beekman' could have been the result of a clerical error in later years."

Sue LaForge took a different attitude: "You know, Chuck, there are quite a few discrepancies in that story, including the exact date of the arrival of Peter Stuyvesant in New Amsterdam." I saw the twinkle in her eye, and I knew she was trying to get some kind of response from Chuck.

"Well, everything around here is so old and so influenced by local versions, that I suppose it is impossible to really pin it down," responded Chuck, "but we do know that a portion of this building was built in 1700, and the site was the crossing of the Kings Highway and a famous Indian trail. This later became the Ulster and Salisbury Turnpike, and a lot of pioneers from Connecticut traveled over it in order to reach New York State."

It's this kind of historical speculation, plus the well-preserved ancient building, that makes the Beekman Arms one of the most visited country inns in the United States. As I've mentioned before, it is a source of friendly argument between Chuck LaForge and Francis Koppeis of Longfellow's Wayside Inn in South Sudbury, Massachusetts, as to just which is the oldest. The real point is that they are both exceptional. I always feel that the trip would be worth it for the food alone — even if there wasn't all that history involved.

Chuck LaForge is a good example of a modern keeper of a country inn who stays completely in touch with contemporary innkeeping trends, while at the same time maintaining the atmosphere that has made the Beekman Arms famous as a stopping place for many presidents, generals, and famous personages during its more than 250 years.

The village of Rhinebeck is one of the loveliest in the Hudson Valley and is within easy driving distance of a great many restored homes and mansions. These include the Vanderbilt Mansion, the Mills Museum, Franklin D. Roosevelt's home, the many buildings connected with Washington's headquarters in Newburg, and Phillipsburg Manor. There are many back roads on both sides of the Hudson.

As we finished dessert at the old hutch table, and Chuck lit a corn cob pipe similar to the kind that have been hanging on some of the heavy beams since 1750, he said: "I'd like to say a few words on behalf of the defense of William Beckman and Peter Stuyvesant. After all, so many arguments have been held in this inn, we might as well continue the tradition."

BEEKMAN ARMS, Rhinebeck, N.Y. 12572; 914-876-7077. A village inn built in 1700. Short drive to F.D.R. Library and Home in Hyde Park. Lodgings. Lunch and dinner served daily, except Christmas. Charles LaForge, Innkeeper.

DE LA VERGNE FARMS, Amenia

De La Vergne Farms, where Rte. 22 (north/south) crosses Route 44 and 343 (east/west) in the center of Amenia, New York, is a 190-year-old building completely restored, with a warm feeling for me the minute I walk in the door. The lobby has deep, comfortable chairs and sofas, and a table with a large wooden bowl filled with shiny red apples. An old clock has been watching travelers for many a decade.

The Dan Patch Room with its beamed ceilings, barn siding, and glowing fireplace sets the pace for a comfortable, candle-lighted, old-fashioned country dinner, with all the trimmings. The menu has real countryside fare — lamb and pork chops, ham, brook trout, local vegetables, fruit pies and your own loaf of bread right from the oven. Incidentally, all the baking is done in the spacious kitchen.

The Peter Pratt Room, another cozy nook, set aside to accommodate the coatless traveler, gives me the sensation of being "back on the farm" as soon as I enter. There is comfortable pine furniture, an old-fashioned chunk stove, and a kerosene lamp. On the other hand, the main dining room gives an elegant touch of yesteryear with handsome wainscoting, colorful matching wallpaper and drapes, polished chandeliers, and carpeted floors.

A few years ago I happened to include in a back edition of CIBR the fact that I had met some young people at De La Vergne Farms who wanted a room for the night without a bath because they thought it would be fun to see what their great-grandfather felt like when he stopped there. In a day when one might think that such conveniences as baths were almost a must in any overnight accommodation, Paul McEnroe has mentioned that there are a suprising number of people who find this type of accommodations at an old country inn rather appealing.

"Of course, almost every one of our rooms has its own bath, but for some people it is a great adventure to 'walk down the hall'."

DE LA VERGNE FARMS, Amenia, N.Y. 12501; 914-373-9141. A village inn at the intersection of Routes 22, 44 & 343 in a delightful rural environment in the Berkshire foothills. About 2 hrs. from NYC. Lodgings. Lunch, dinner served daily except Tuesday. Closed for winter vacation. Always telephone in advance. Paul McEnroe, Innkeeper.

SWISS HUTTE, Hillsdale

It was a very bright, very cold, blowy Saturday afternoon in January. I was at the Swiss Hutte for a spot of lunch and a chat with Tom and Linda Breen. They were telling me about their new boat which they now keep in

Catamount ski area

the Bahamas and try to use at least two and a half months of each year.

I sat in a warm, sunny corner with the panorama of the Catamount Ski Area spread out before me. It was a little too cold to ski, and there were quite a few people who stopped for lunch. There was a great deal of kidding about going back on the slopes in the afternoon.

This same scene is quite different in the middle of the summer with the rushing brook gurgling its way down the mountain and the natural swimming pool out in front of the inn with people sunning themselves.

Oddly enough, the people who were here today were almost as tan and ruddy as the summer guests.

The Swiss Hutte is a continental-type inn in a hidden Berkshire valley right on the New York-Massachusetts line. It is actually in Hillsdale, New York, but I can't help but think of it as being a Massachusetts inn. The chalet-type accommodations are very popular with the skiers because of the adjacency to the slopes. In the summer everything feels sequestered among the trees.

Coming up the Taconic Parkway from New York it is an ideal distance to leave late in the afternoon and arrive for dinner. Even today there was a variety of license plates in the parking lot, including California and West Virginia.

In spite of all this natural beauty, perhaps the Swiss Hutte is best known for its food. Both lunch and dinner are leisurely affairs with individually prepared dishes. That particular day I ordered duckling livers in Madeira. The cool, fresh salad was delicately bathed in a perfect combination of oil and vinegar and condiments. The fresh French bread was hot to the touch.

Among the evening entrees are chicken curry, Dover sole, Toranadoes of Beef and sweetbreads.

Desserts, which are included with your dinner entree, are delicious French Napoleons that are made fresh and many other homemade creamy pastries.

The seasons may change, but the Swiss Hutte food remains delightful at all times.

SWISS HUTTE, Hillsdale, N.Y. 12529; 518-325-3333. An Alpine country inn 6 mi. from Gt. Barrington, Mass. and 10 mi. east of Taconic Pkwy. on Rte. 23. Mod. American Plan in winter; European Plan in summer. Lodgings. Breakfast, lunch, dinner served to travelers. Open every day except months of April and Nov. Tom and Linda Breen, Innkeepers.

BULL'S HEAD INN, Cobleskill

It was dusk and the clock in front of the Bull's Head showed five o'clock on an early December's evening. The red flame on the torch in front of the inn was already becoming more visible. There was the air of expectancy that seems to precede the Christmas holidays as some of the Christmas lights were already lit in the Cobleskill stores and shops.

The big door opened as I ventured up the walk. There stood Monty Allen as dapper as ever, with a big smile of welcome. In the background I could see Shirley coming forward.

"Come on in," he said. "We have time before people start coming in to have a little visit. Where have you been traveling recently, Berkshire Traveller?"

It's a funny thing, I hadn't seen Monty and Shirley for almost a year, and yet both of them are so genuinely warm that we started talking like we'd left off almost the day before. I explained that I was doing a tour of some

of the New York State inns including the Old Red Mill
in Buffalo, the Glen Iris in Castile, the Springside Inn in
Auburn and the Lincklaen House in Cazenovia.

"Oh, we've got to get over and see Helen," said
Shirley. "It's such a pretty drive on Rte. 20."

Things hadn't changed much at the Bull's Head, except for a few more old farm implements and artifacts
which the Allens' friends had presented to them since
my last visit. There was a new hay rake, a lantern and
another picture of early Cobleskill. Another thing that
brought me right back was the marvelous aroma from the
open hearth in the back of the dining room where Chef
Schaeffer was already starting on the beef specialties of
the evening. Monty said that the tenderloin with Bordelaise sauce, the filet mignon and the ribs continue to be
the thing that people ask for again and again. He indicated   these and other beef dishes on the clever wooden
menu which has been a feature of the inn.

"I hope you make it clear to your readers that we
don't have lodgings here," he said. "We're happy to direct
people to where there are some clean, adequate accommodations nearby."

The Bull's Head is a hearty restaurant in the heartland of the rich central New York State farming country. Many visitors find it an interesting experience to visit nearby Howe Caverns as well.

People were now coming in for dinner and Monty suggested that we order. After all these years of ordering the tenderloin with Bordelaise, I broke precedent and ordered the charcoal broiled filet.

BULL'S HEAD INN, 2 Park Pl., Cobleskill, N.Y. 12043; 518-234-3591. A restaurant on Rte. 7 about 5 mi. west from Howe Caverns. Lunch served Tues. and Thurs., Dinner Tues. — Sat., Sun. 1 PM — 8 PM.. Closed Mon. and Christmas Day. No lodgings. Monty and Shirley Allen, Innkeepers.

LINCKLAEN HOUSE, Cazenovia

Helen Tobin is absolutely unbelievable. She is the keeper of an excellent village inn in Cazenovia, New York; raises a family; always full of beans and good humor; and yet always seems to be able to take time to talk at length with her guests.

I love to drop in unexpectedly on her, and she never disappoints me. She makes everyone feel like they are the only people in the world. She was about to have lunch with two of her guests, Nancy and George Jackson from Farmington, Connecticut, who explained that they come each year for a bit of "relaxed skiing." They invited me to have lunch with them, and since there was a dance being held at the inn that evening, we went into one of the little side dining rooms that had a merry fire in an imposing fireplace with a brass fender around it. It was an early December weekend with a considerable amount of early snow. The inn was decorated for Christmas and there was an air of holiday expectancy about it.

Lunch was a buffet with all kinds of hot and cold goodies, but I had eyes only for the hot popovers, which are served at all Lincklaen House meals. Between bites, Helen called my attention to the new antique-red carpet, dyed to be compatible with the ivory-toned wood panelled walls and ceiling. My eyes were drawn to the end of the room where another fireplace was sending forth a cheery greeting.

Cazenovia library

It is truly an elegant dining room, one reminiscent of the 18th century French townhouse from which the Lincklaen was copied. Conte de Cazenovia, for whom the village is named, lived in Lyons, France. Rumor has it he was an agent to arrange for disposing of the land of a French refugee from Napoleon who later became Charles X of France and who built a fortress on extensive holdings a few miles south of Cazenovia. This fortress stood until the 1920's, when it burned. The story is told in the book, "Muller's Hill," written by a local author.

There were quite a few parents at lunch who had come to Cazenovia to pick up students at Cazenovia Junior College.

Helen was most enthusiastic about the fact that the Lorenzo State Museum would soon be open in Cazenovia.

At dinner that night I learned a new outdoor patio would be ready this coming spring. 'The Lincklaen House is L-shaped, and the patio will be inside the 'L' away from the street," Helen explained. "We'll put in a hedge and use potted plants to screen the little tables. I was inspired by the garden patio of Mrs. Munson's Lamothe House, a family home she opened to the public in New Orleans. Cazenovia has lovely gardens and I want my guests to enjoy mine," Helen said.

With Helen Tobin, Cazenovia's 19th century grace is being preserved.

LINCKLAEN HOUSE, Cazenovia, N.Y. 13035; 315-655-3461. A village inn on Rte. 20 (Cherry Valley Tpke.), 18 mi. east of Syracuse just south of the N.Y. Thrwy. Lodgings. Breakfast, lunch, dinner served daily. Alpine ski. Helen Tobin, Innkeeper.

SPRINGSIDE INN, Auburn

I received a letter from Bill and Barbara Dove at the Springside Inn in Auburn, New York. Part of it read this way:

"We've had another excellent year here at Springside. The Sunday brunch you wrote about in the last edition has continued to be one of the most popular meals we serve. We found that the scrambled eggs, hash browned potatoes and ham hash had to be replenished frequently.

"The Springside Summer Theatre had another exciting season and it looks as though we will be doing it again this year. Our professional staff company will be back and it is the only dinner theatre in the area.

"We had some very enthusiastic people traveling with 'Country Inns and Back Roads' and I thought you'd be interested in knowing more about some of the places that we direct them to in the vicinity. For example: There is our reconstructed Cayuga Indian Village at the end of Owasco Lake. This is open from June 25th to September 1st.

"We also have the home of Harriet Tubman, the black leader who organized the underground railroad for slaves in this area and used Springside Inn as one of the slave hiding places.

"We have the Seward Museum which is located adjacent to the Auburn City Hall. Seward, as you know, was Secretary of State during the Lincoln Administration and was responsible for purchasing Alaska. The first year this acquisition produced more in furs alone than the original purchase price. John D. Rockefeller was born in the town of Niles near Moravia which is about a 25 minute drive from the inn. The house is marked.

"Millard Filmore's reconstructed home is located at Filmore Glen State Park, a picturesque gorge at the southern tip of Owasco Lake. The area is available for picnics from June 1st to September 30th, and we send quite a few guests down there with a box lunch.

"So you see, not only do we have a large area of the Finger Lakes themselves, which has waterfalls, glens, ravines, beaches, lagoons and twelve state parks, but there are quite a few other historically-oriented sites nearby. We discovered that many of our guests coming across the New York State Thruway stay on an extra day.

"Our people can leave the New York Thruway at the Weedsport exit #40 and drive south directly through Auburn, and we are just minutes away, on Owasco Lake.

"By the way, you will be interested in knowing that our popovers are even more in demand than ever since you mentioned them in the book. I think we are one of the few places in our vicinity that actually have popover ovens.

"I thought of you the other day when we had a wedding party here at the inn and the bride stood at the top of the little staircase and threw her bouquet to her friends. You have always said that the stairway would make a lovely setting, and it does.

"We are looking forward to your visit again this year. Best wishes, Bill and Barbara Dove."

SPRINGSIDE INN, 41 West Lake Rd., Auburn, N.Y. 13021; 315-252-7247. A country inn on Rte. 38S, 3 mi. south of Auburn with a view af Owasco Lake. In the heart of the beautiful and historical Finger Lakes. (From N.Y. State Thwy. exit at Weedsport #40). Lodgings. Mod. American Plan available. Dinner served daily to travelers except Monday. Closed Memorial Day, July 4th, Christmas and New Years Day. Bill and Barbara Dove, Innkeepers.

Genesee River Falls at Letchworth State Park

GLEN IRIS INN, Castile

"Today at least you can hear yourself," said Peter Pizzutelli, as we walked the few steps from the front of the Glen Iris Inn to a lookout point on the Genesee River where the falls are 107 feet high.

"However, during the flood in June the sound was absolutely awesome. A roar that just defies description."

Peter was talking about the great rainfall and floods which followed during the early part of the summer of 1972. It seemed quite remote during this lovely summer day in the early part of August; the river had gone down considerably, although there was still a tremendous a- mount of water going over the great falls.

I have visited the Glen Iris in Letchworth State Park many times. The inn is very well run and has excellent food and most comfortable lodgings. It is impossible to separate it from this truly beautiful state park which never fails to evoke a feeling of grateful wonder because of its great natural beauties. The park is in western New York State, south of Rochester, and is a patch of green about 18 miles long and a few miles wide on most of the service station maps. The original one thousand acres was donated by William Pryor Letchworth, whose home was in the building which is now the inn.

The Genesee River has been slicing its way between the high banks creating deeper channels with every mil- lennium. The entire region is rich in geological lore and was also a significant area inhabited by members of the Six Nations, a group of Indian tribes in Western New York State.

The road, which traverses the length of the park, comes very close to the river and in several places extremely well designed lookout points have been established. The park abounds in small game, and one of the oddities is that woodchucks are protected by law because the Park Commissioners felt that this was the most accessible animal for small children to see in their natural habitat.

"It is hard to imagine a more marvelous setting for a country inn," I remarked, as Peter and I walked back to the broad green lawns where so many weddings take place each summer. We threaded our way between the tall pine trees, and now and then the morning sunlight caught a flash of color as the birds flitted from tree to tree. Everything in and around the inn was beautifully cared for, with many evergreen shrubs and ferns and brilliant flowers.

This is the Glen Iris Inn, a most unusual country inn.

GLEN IRIS INN, Castile, N.Y. 14427; 716-493-2622. A country inn located at the Falls of the Genesee, 55 mi. from Buffalo and Rochester off Rtes. 39, 19A and 436 in Letchworth State Park. Lodgings. Breakfast, lunch, dinner served daily from Easter Sunday through first full weekend in November. Peter and Cora Pizzutelli, Innkeepers.

OLD RED MILL, Clarence

It was snowing. It snows frequently and vigorously in western New York State. I had been driving across the New York State Thruway and after following the directions in CIBR, in no time at all I found myself approaching the Old Red Mill with a great deal of anticipation. It may have been the heavy snow collecting on the mill wheel, or the red sleigh on the roof, but I had a holiday feeling.

After warm greetings, I followed Innkeeper Bob Lenz through the dining rooms which were now filling up with hungry guests, and we stepped out into what I thought was going to be the railroad caboose which Bob had acquired a few years ago. However, instead to my surprise, there was a full-fledged Union Pacific Dining Car, vintage circa 1910. The red carpets and the carmine-glassed swinging lamps and furnishings were just as if Leland Stanford himself might walk in at any moment.

When I gathered my wits about me I asked, "Where is the caboose?" He answered, "Oh, we moved that over to the other side of the building."

Bob Lenz is a most resourceful and inventive innkeeper. One of the very first things he did when he acquired this building was to fill the walls with farm and shop implements and tools that were used in western New York during the last of the century. It is one of the

Railroading mementos

most impressive collections outside of a museum. Then came the caboose, and now the dining car.

But the piece de resistance was yet to come. When I asked to see the menu he handed me a reproduction of an old-time railroad ticket that had all of the offerings printed in little boxes around the outside, and when I selected I simply punched a hole next to the dish that I had chosen. I punched a New York state strip steak (14 oz.) which was cooked medium rare (as I had requested). It was right on time on the main track!

I picked up a little table tent that said that "Country Inns and Back Roads" and the "Country Inn Cookbook" were for sale at the main desk. However, on the other side there was a collection of rather interesting aphorisms which might apply to many situations in our daily life. For example: "A man without mirth is like a wagon without springs . . . he is jolted disagreeably by every pebble in the road."

Resourceful Bob said that it was quite surprising how many people took these along as a souvenir of their visit. As he remarked: "I'm happy to say that many of them are buying 'Country Inns and Back Roads' as well."

OLD RED MILL, Clarence, N.Y. (mailing address: 8326 Main St., Williamsville, N.Y. 14221); 716-633-7878. A country restaurant on Rte. 5, one quarter mile east of Rte. 78; 16 mi. from Buffalo. Lunch Mon.-Fri., dinner served daily except December 24th and 25. Robert Lenz, Innkeeper.

CLARKSON HOUSE, Lewiston

A light snow was falling on an early December evening when I first visited the Clarkson House in Lewiston, New York. The Christmas tree lights were already out blinking their happy message, and there was a small group of figures depicting the Holy Family across from the inn. I ventured down the street to see the appealing miniature Christmas tree lights draped around each of the trees in the business district, and it all made a very happy holiday effect.

For me this was the first visit to this corner of New York State which is dominated by the presence of Niagara Falls. I learned about the Clarkson House from my good friend and innkeeper, Robert Lenz of the Old Red Mill in Williamsville. Bob said that it was very special, and he proved to be right.

First of all, in addition to the Falls, I soon realized that this area was influenced by the happenings of the War of 1812. There was a battle along the Niagara River between the United States and Canada, and the British burned Lewiston, N.Y. to the ground on the cold night of December 19, 1813. Innkeeper Bob Clarkson has a small cannonball on display at the inn which a Canadian customer gave him a few years ago saying: "This was one of yours that was sent over during the war of 1812 and I am returning it." It's a real cannonball.

Niagara Falls

I found the Clarkson House to be an excellent resturant—something I felt almost instinctively as I sensed the delicious aroma. There are several most unusual features with a great deal of emphasis on small details that make it exceptional.

I discovered that the reason for the enchanting aroma was the fact that the charcoal grill is right in the middle of the dining area, and the filets and lamb chops were sizzling away merrily. Around it, there is an eccentric arrangement of booths and tables, and on the walls a collection of tools and gadgets used more than 100 years ago. They haven't discovered the use for some of them! There are old-fashion-

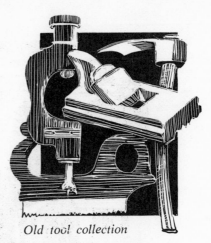

Old tool collection

ed kerosene lamps on the tables, and the walls have several good paintings interspersed with wall lamps.

On that first trip I discovered that Bob Clarkson is a great believer in having things under control. For example, there are only 22 tables, all carefully spaced out on the wooden floor which is scrubbed every day. This means that reservations are most advisable as there are a limited number of diners that can be accommodated.

Secondly, the menu has been carefully limited to a few entrees which are very carefully prepared and most tastefully arranged on the plates. There is an emphasis on beef, including sirloin, filet and prime rib. There are also delicious French-cut lamb chops. In addition, there is a combination of beef filet and lobster tail, or a half of a Maine lobster (flown in fresh).

That, plus four desserts, including cherries jubilee and baked Alaska, is the menu. I mustn't forget to mention that there was a little sign on one of those delicious-looking baked potatoes that said: "Eat all of me if you like, I've been scrubbed and tubbed."

I thoroughly enjoyed my dinner at the Clarkson House. It would be a great place even if Niagara Falls were somewhere else.

CLARKSON HOUSE, 810 Center St., Lewiston, N.Y. 14092; 716-754-4544. A country restaurant on Rte. 18F, 7 mi. from Niagara Falls and 7 mi. from Fort Niagara. No lodgings. Dinner served every day except Mondays. Closed Christmas. Bob and Marilyn Clarkson, Innkeepers.

Beach on Fourth Lake

MOHAWK INN, Old Forge

It was near sunset. I walked from the tennis courts down to the beach on the path in front of the neat little lodges with Indian names such as Cherokee, Algonquin and Jutowesta. There were a number of small children playing in the sand on the lakeshore. Overhead there was tier after tier of billowy clouds in the azure sky. In the foreground a few people were getting ready to take a twilight boatride, and in the background the lake stretched out into the blue-green distant shores.

This was The Mohawk, on Fourth Lake in the middle of the Adirondack vastness. I had heard about it from several helpful readers, and I only wish that I had gotten there a year earlier. Some of the guests that I chatted with had been returning for the last forty years.

"This is just a wonderful place for children," explained one mother to me. "There is a children's hostess, and a very good program of activities for them besides the things we do together as a family. For instance, we bring our boat. The children learned how to swim here as well as water ski, and I've never really tasted such good food. My mother and father brought me here on the train 30 years ago."

I believe The Mohawk can best be described as a family vacation resort inn. Besides the waterfront and hiking activities, there is a program every evening for guests who want to participate. These include movies, dancing, games, special entertainment and special events. Perhaps the most attractive aspect is the clear, fresh air and soft cool breezes from the lakes and evergreen forests. In our own lodge at the water's edge, I found it very easy to find serenity and peace of mind.

It's quite easy to understand why Robert Fulton became so enamored of this chain of lakes. Later they became known as "Fulton's Lakes."

A word or two about the food at The Mohawk. I saved my menu from the evening meal and among the American Plan choices were broiled steak, roast fresh ham with brown gravy and applesauce and scallops sauteed in a wine sauce. There was also some excellent fresh cauliflower with lemon butter, hot rolls and a choice of five desserts including a piece of Brandy Alexander pie, which is made with graham cracker crust.

Small wonder, indeed, that my new found friend said that her sons return from their vacation at The Mohawk "as brown and round as a berry."

MOHAWK INN, COUNTRY AND BOAT CLUB, Fourth Lake, Old Forge, N.Y. 13420; 315-357-2491. An Adirondack resort inn on Rte. 28, 8 mi. north of Old Forge. Lodgings. American, Mod. American and European Plan. Breakfast, lunch, dinner served to travelers. Open mid-June to mid-Oct. Margaret and Allen Wilcox, Innkeepers.

On my previous trip from Bridgeport to Port Jefferson, I had failed to estimate the time properly and was not able to get my car on the ferry, so I went over as a passenger. This time, I arrived in Bridgeport to find I had enough time to get lost a couple of times trying to find the ferry slip, but still had ample time to make certain that my car would be included.

There is another ferry from New London to Orient Point, which although I have never taken it, looks like a very sensible way to reach Long Island from New England without going all the way into the city.

THREE VILLAGE INN, Stony Brook

Oh boy, the sweet aroma of the salt marshes, the swooping gulls, the unique sight of so many boats all neatly tucked away at their moorings, and a fresh breeze from the Sound in my face! Why had I spent all my life as an inland sod-buster, instead of running away to sea when I was 14?

I was back for a second visit at the Three Village Inn, and it was every bit as enticing as the first time, plus a few extras that I had missed. I had already checked out a few of my first impressions such as the Carriage Museum, the yacht club marina just behind the inn, the eagle that flaps his wings at 12 o'clock, and the carved head of Hercules.

From carriage museum

Oddly enough, a few days earlier, a visitor to my Book Stall in Stockbridge remarked that he just never expected to find such a perfect place as the III V I so close to the City.

"I had one of those little cottages that look out over the yacht club," he said. "My wife and I went down on a Saturday night, as per your suggestion, stayed an extra two days and then went back later on."

In addition to the rather quiet and subdued atmosphere, he also made a point about the food.

"They do something I've never seen before," he said. "They serve sherbet with the main course. At one particular meal I had the flounder stuffed with seafood, and the sherbet was exactly the right touch of sweet and moistener."

I learned one interesting development since my previous visit, and that is that Nelson and Monda Roberts' son Whitney is most actively involved in the keeping of the inn. As Monda said, "He grew up right here." He is a very enthusiastic young man with a great deal of zest for the business. Actually, it is a business that ought to attract many young people. Country inn-keeping is personal and real.

Monda reminded me that I had made a vague promise about visiting the inn on Thanksgiving last year, and then went on to tell me what a really gala affair it always is — complete with members of the staff in special costumes, special table decorations and unusual extras on the menu.

"I know that you would just love it," she said.

I made another vague promise to visit on the next Thanksgiving. However, in reality, it is fun to go to the Three Village Inn at anytime.

THREE VILLAGE INN, Dock Rd., Stony Brook, L.I., N.Y. 11790; 516-751-0555. A village inn, ½ mi. north of Rte. 25A, 5 mi. from Port Jefferson, L.I. on Long Island's historic north shore. Many historical and natural attractions nearby. Lodgings. Lunch and dinner served daily. Nelson and Monda Roberts, Innkeepers.

New Jersey

New Jersey is rich in Colonial and Revolutionary history. Near the scene of the Battle of Monmouth in Freehold there is a bustling village inn, and in Cranbury, an inn that was flourishing during the Battles of Princeton and Trenton.

CRANBURY INN, Cranbury

Anton Bremec, the new innkeeper of the Cranbury Inn, proved to be most knowledgeable on the subject of the history of Cranbury and its environs.

"In 1776, after Washington had retreated from New York across New Jersey just in front of General Howe's soldiers, his army passed through Princeton and then crossed the Delaware. It looked pretty bad, but then he re-crossed the Delaware and attacked the Hessians at Trenton on Christmas night, 1776. He also beat the enemy at Princeton and then went to a more favorable defensive position in northern New Jersey — Morristown."

An old Cranbury landmark, Brainerd Institute

The Cranbury Inn was built during those difficult days. At that time it was known as the Post House, and it was a stage stop between New York and Philadelphia. The name was changed around 1780 to the United States Hotel in a burst of patriotic feeling.

As if to underscore our interesting conversation, my eye caught the collection of antique firearms assembled during the past few years at the Cranbury Inn. It includes dueling pistols, flintlocks, shotguns, and ancient ball ammunition. Many of these are mounted on the walls in handsome cases. There is also a large collection of old plates placed around the old beams, along with prints and oil paintings of Colonial figures. One wall is covered by a painting showing passengers on the South Amboy-Bordentown Stage alighting for sustenance at the inn over a century ago.

Both the luncheon and dinner menus are chock-full of country favorites, many of them associated with New Jersey. They feature real south Jersey turkey, soft-shell crab, shrimp, duckling, king crab, and oysters. Today, the wide variety of truck farms in New Jersey supply fresh vegetables throughout most of the year for this excellent country restaurant.

One of the memorable features about visiting the Cranbury Inn is the village of Cranbury itself. It has quiet, shaded streets with many white Colonial buildings, as well as a sprinkling of impressive Victorian structures, one of which Jan has sketched above. It has a most restful and peaceful environment.

Situated as it is off Exit 6A on the New Jersey Turnpike, I found it is an excellent distance from both New York and Philadelphia to enjoy a most leisurely meal. Pity it has no lodgings.

CRANBURY INN, 21 S. Main St., Cranbury, N.J. 08512; 609-395-0609. A country restaurant on the Old King George Hwy. Cranbury is 9 mi. east of Princeton near Monmouth and Princeton Revolutionary War battlefields. Lunch and dinner served every day except Monday and Christmas. No lodgings. Anton Bremec; Richard Zanyor, Innkeepers.

AMERICAN HOTEL, Freehold

The little sign said "the horseiest place in New Jersey." Augie Daesener chuckled, "Well I guess that's true; we love horses."

I looked around and readily agreed, however, I saw many evidences of the American Hotel being guest-oriented as well. There is a feeling of warmth and caring. The lobby has big comfortable chairs and sofas arranged for long hours of conversation and the perusal of scratch sheets; and welcoming new arrivals and exchanging words with old friends is Augie Daesener, the innkeeper.

This devotion to the horse and to the "improving of the breed" is indigenous with the fact that Freehold is the location of Freehold Raceway, and Monmouth Park is also nearby. In fact, Augie chimed in with the news that the original starting bell from Monmouth Park is at the inn.

In addition to this very horsey environment, it is just a few minutes from the inn to Monmouth Battlefield, where the famous Molly Pitcher brought water to the striving soldiers of the American Revolutionary War.

The newest addition to the inn is the Williamsburg Room, a dining room inspired by the famous Virginia restoration. It has excellent oils hung on the panelled walls, and the entire atmosphere is one of 18th century elegance.

Monument at Monmouth Battlefield

Foodwise, the proximity to the Jersey shore makes the American Hotel Seafood Platter one of the most desirable of experiences. It includes shrimp, scallops, flounder, and other fish in season. I'm sure there is never any grease, and bread crumbs are never used!

However, I wouldn't want to leave anyone with the impression that the American Hotel is essentially a seafood place—it has one of the largest and most varied menus I've ever seen. Augie takes great pride in the fact that he is able to offer so many different entrees. "You know, we have such a wide variety of people who stop off to see us, that we are prepared to serve most anything within reason," he said.

Although the rooms at the American Hotel are a bit on the plain side, I was very happy to enjoy a good night's sleep after a day of backroading in history and antiquing in that section of New Jersey. It is a place where real country inns are few and far between.

AMERICAN HOTEL, 18 E. Main St., Freehold, N.J. 07728; 201-462-0819. On Rte. 9, midway between Garden State Pkwy. and N.J. Tpks., 50 mi. from N.Y. A country inn with clean and modest lodgings in a bustling Jersey town. Open every day in the year for breakfast, lunch and dinner. Augie Daesener, Innkeeper.

Pennsylvania

Since our last edition we have discovered two new country inns in Pennsylvania. One to the south of Harrisburg near the Maryland border not far from Waynesboro. The other in Bucks County, just north of New Hope.

Speaking of Bucks County, this region has some of the
most historically oriented back roads in America. There
is a widely distributed brochure of the region called
"Highways of History" which is a help. I was glad that
I stopped for a few moments at the restored village of
Fallsington which is just west of Morrisville off of the
Lincoln Highway (US 1). The stone buildings, quiet at-
mosphere and gentle air of the 18th century are quite an
experience. There is famous back roading in Pennsylvania
in the Lancaster County area where there are the farms
of the Amish and other "plain people."

I also had occasion recently to travel along sections
of Route 6 across the northern part of the state through
some old towns like Wellsboro, Allaghany and Warren.
So far no inns in this part of the state.

1740 HOUSE, Lumberville

I left my beret at the 1740 House. Harry Nessler
said, as he saw me stuffing it into my pocket, "Oh, no,
just put it there on the coat rack, you'll remember it." I
realize now what sheer folly his advice was. For the next
few hours my mind would be a-whirl with the myriad of
delightful details concerning my visit. This is the inn for
which I had seen the advertisements in the New Yorker
that read: "If you can't be a house guest in Bucks County,
be ours." Harry finally won me over.

I arrived after dark in time for dinner, thank heavens.
I took the long way from Philadelphia, following the
river road from south of Washington's Crossing through
New Hope.

Harry and Janet Nessler proved to be two lovely
people. Everything about this rambling riverside inn reflects her exquisite taste and his uncanny attention to
detail. I'm sure that it will take several editions of this
book to really cover them all.

I looked at several different rooms, all of which had
harmoniously selected country furniture and decorations
and each had its own balcony. For example, I chose an
old stable, three walls of which were of heavy stone

quarried from the Delaware cliffs at least 100 years ago. A marvelously huge window overlooked (as do all the rooms) both the canal and the river with the swaying trees appearing to beckon for a closer look. On another side the windows overlooked the modest swimming pool which is heated even during the winter when a light mist rises from its surface.

After dinner and a long talk with the Nesslers and their guests in the panelled living room, I selected a book from the spacious library and discovered upon my return to my room that the night maid had turned down my bed!

A word or two should be mentioned about my dinner. I had roast glazed duck, the memory of which still makes my mouth water. The broccoli had an unusual seasoning, and the potatoes were something special too. I also sampled the beef Bourguignonne—it was delicious. The brick-floored dining room, which also overlooks the river, has a profusion of climbing flowers which are trained around the windows. The entire atmosphere is one of warmth.

By the way, a buffet breakfast is served every morning, and you have your choice of fruit juice, cold cereals, croissants, danish, jams and marmalades, hot hard boiled eggs, coffee or tea. You serve yourself — as often as you want.

It was at dinner that I heard another guest remark, "This is the most romantic country inn I have ever visited."

I'm purposely leaving my beret at the 1740 House. It will insure my early return to retrieve it!

1740 HOUSE, River Rd., Lumberville, Pa. 18933; 215-297-5661. A riverside inn on Rte. 32, 6½ miles north of New Hope, Pa. in the heart of historical Bucks County. Lodgings. European Plan. Dinners served to travelers by reservation only Tues. through Sat. Continental Breakfast served to house guests. Open all year. Janet and Harry Nessler, Innkeepers.

PUMP HOUSE INN, Canadensis

Question: Can a twenty-year-old boy with his mind on skiing, food, rock music and foreign sports cars bridge the generation gap and find happiness with his father for a weekend at a country inn? That's a pretty tall order, but it happened with my son, Keith, and me at the Pump House Inn.

It was mid-afternoon when we, after driving up from the Park View Inn in northeast West Virginia, drove in to the parking lot at the Pump House. The first thing that caught Keith's eye was a red Ferrari. "Oh, boy!"

Frankly, I don't believe he thought this was the real "way out" way to spend a weekend, but I did hope that he would be willing to consider a new situation. As we drove through the Poconos on our way north to Canadensis, he remarked that it seemed there were an unusual number of ski areas. "I remember when maybe there were one or two," he said, "but now there are at least eight or nine. That's pretty convenient for people who want to get out of the city. This is beautiful country."

Todd Drucquer, after greeting us with his usual charm, really came on big with Keith. Although Todd is married with two growing youngsters, he really is not that much older, and easily drew Keith into conversation. I'd seen the inn before so Todd showed him around the kitchens, the wine cellar, the dining rooms and the Pub with its log-burning fireplace.

Meanwhile I had a chance to talk with Henri and Shirley, Todd's father and mother, about some of the exciting things that had been going on. The Pump House is really a family affair with a very good mixture of ideas being exchanged.

"I think one of the most significant moves we have made this year was to send Todd, always ready to absorb new ideas and meet other innkeepers, on a study tour of his own to visit other country inns in the Mid-Atlantic and Southern states. At the same time we sent our chef, Bill Cardwell, to Europe last fall to do further research on the foods of France and Switzerland to enrich our own present menu, although we are very well known for French provincial specialties already.

"Ten years ago when Shirley and I came to the mountains and saw this old farmhouse built in 1842 we fell in love with it and hoped that Todd would join us in running a country inn. He agreed with enthusiasm to join us in our endeavor. Who could dream that our small inn would come to this?"

Later we all joined for dinner in the dining room with its own natural indoor waterfall. The houseguest who owned the red Ferrari gave Keith the keys and told him to take a spin. He came back and said that it handled almost as well as a Porsche.

As we were turning in for the night after a really exciting evening, Keith cast his vote: "You know, Dad, they've really got it all together here!"

THE PUMP HOUSE INN, Canadensis, Pennsylvania 18325; 717-595-7501. A country inn on Route 390N (Skytop Road) 1½ miles north of Canadensis village. Located high in the Poconos, 18 miles northeast of Stroudsburg (I-80). Near ski areas, golf courses, summer theatre. Lodgings (with Continental breakfast). Sophisticated country dining year 'round. Closed December 1-25. The Drucquer Family, Innkeepers.

CANDLEWYCK INN, Green Lane

I always enjoy lunch at the Candlewyck. For one thing, it gives me a chance to wander around the property including the sedate old Pennsylvania barn which has been livened up by a number of hex signs, a formidable pond with much wildlife, and a beautiful gift shop.

However, to arrive after nightfall has a very special meaning for me. There is the huge candle, which is really an old silo, that can be seen for miles in the distance.

Pennsylvania Dutch barn

The approach is further enhanced by the gentle flood lighting of the old, whitewashed building. I turn into the drive among the fruit trees and this is where I first see the flickers of at least 135 candles which provide the main lighting throughout the inn.

I've known Bob and Dotty Smith for a number of years. They have a knack for not only running a rare country inn, but for being able to make literally hundreds of guests feel that they are somebody very special.

This so-called "knack" of which I spoke, is really a very light way to say that they possess a great deal of experience and organizing ability. This now involves a rapidly enlarging family. Bob and Dotty started all of this a number of years ago by taking an old farmhouse and completely rehabilitating it. They are now re-enforced by enthusiastic young people who are really running this whole show.

At one time during a recent visit for dinner I found myself surrounded by Mr. and Mrs. Rober Schwind (the Smith's daughter and her husband, both active in the inn) as well as the Smith's son, Bob, who is the principal chef. A number of grandchildren were introduced — it looked like an invasion of Smith relatives.

One of the things about which everyone is proud is the unusual number of newspaper clippings with favorable editorial comments by food editors from the Philadelphia area.

Chef Robert suggested that this time I have the Candlewyck Sportsman, which is a small filet and lobster tail combination. He recommended this just about the time my eye had stopped on the chicken Boissiere, chicken stuffed with mushrooms and herbs and topped with a special sauce. It is a well known fact that I can never resist the tenderloin tips Robert!

The dilemma was solved by Bob having one, Dotty having another, and I having the third — and we all shared. It will work everytime.

Besides the good food, good service, and good fun which everyone can enjoy at the Candlewyck, I am particularly grateful for the available lodging rooms. It suits my purpose to stay on each evening and rise early in the morning in that wonderful, fresh Perkiomen Valley air, and getting an early start to my next country inn.

CANDLEWYCK INN, Green Lane, Pa. 18054; 215-679-2998. A country inn 17 mi. from Allentown on Rt. 29 in the rich Perkiomen Valley near Green Lane Park and Fishery. Lodgings. European Plan. Lunch and dinner served daily except Monday. Closed Christmas Day and New Years Day. Alpine skiing. Smith Family, Innkeepers.

KIMBERTON COUNTRY HOUSE, Kimberton

The birds were singing and the ducks were on the pond. We walked past the Village Bookstore, the Yarn Shop, and the Pantry, all housed in an ancient stone building with that wonderful Pennsylvania fieldstone patina. It seemed hardly possible that downtown Philadelphia was a short 45 minutes away! This was, indeed, a sheltered enclave of Chester County's past. Valley Forge is just about 6 miles away, and Brandywine Battlefield is a few miles to the south.

The Kimberton Inn was originally built in 1796 to accommodate the parents who were visiting their daughters attending an adjacent private school. The school itself was contained in the original buildings that now have the shops mentioned earlier. Much of the pastoral quality of the old crossroads has been well preserved, and there is hardly a hint of modern intrusion.

"Light and airy" might be the description of the main dining room where I had lunched earlier. It overlooks the mill pond and water wheel, and the white ceilings and heavy brown-stained beams are very pleasant to the eye. The older sections of the inn, which date well into the early part of the 19th century, have quite low ceilings and a fine collection of sabres, pewterware, and eagles on the wall. Much of the flooring in this section is of beautiful red brick.

The menu at the Kimberton, which incidentally has no lodging rooms, has a wide choice of seafood such as lobster tail, flounder, shrimp, scallops, etc. There are also steak sirloin Pizzaiola and chicken Kiev, just to name a few. Each time I'm there I have an extra helping of sticky buns that are baked fresh daily.

Lee and Francis Slobodzian have worked diligently for many years, carefully adding to the dimensions of the Kimberton Country House. Some of the little things that mean so much are the flowers which are personally grown by Leon in his own hothouse. Another interesting feature is the gift shop which has grown considerably since the first time I saw it a number of years ago. This is Francis' department and she has thoughtfully arranged for replicas of many attractive lamps, candle holders, and dishes in the dining room to be available. Small wonder that the birds sing at the Kimberton Country House.

KIMBERTON COUNTRY HOUSE, Kimberton, Pa. 19442; 215-933-8148. A Colonial restaurant in a preserved 18th century crossroads, 6 mi. from Valley Forge State Park. Presently accessible via the Pa. Turnpike, Valley Forge Exit Rte. 113 near Phoenixville. Dinner daily, except Mondays and Christmas. Leon and Francis Slobodzian, Innkeepers.

MOSELEM SPRINGS INN, Moselem Springs

I believe that it was in 1967 on a rather rainy night when I found my way to the outer reaches of Berks County in Pennsylvania to visit the Moselem Springs Inn for the first time. Since that time the flaming gas lamps on the broad porch have warmed my welcome again and again.

In those days the Moselem Springs Inn was the furthest inn to the west that we included in our book. It hardly seems possible now, since we've extended our travels beyond the borders of Pennsylvania to Michigan, Illinois, and even to California. But at that time, it was really quite an adventure.

During the ensuing years I have received a number of letters from readers praising Moselem Springs. However, none of them means more to me than one that says

in part: "The Moselem Springs Inn was the highlight of our trip. Everything was perfect. Mr. and Mrs. Stoudt were out of town, but the warmth and hospitality they have created was there in their absence. It was nice to find a menu with such new and interesting items."

We receive complimentary letters like this every day from people who visit the various inns, and certainly Moselem Springs has had quite a few. This particular letter, however, came from Robert Lenz who is the inn-keeper of the Old Red Mill Inn in Williamsville, N.Y. (which is also included in "Country Inns and Back Roads"), so that it was a particular delight for me to have my opinion supported by one of our knowledgeable innkeepers.

Curiously enough, Moselem Springs Inn is closed on Saturdays because of Walter and Madeline Stoudt's religious convictions. However, it is open on Sunday and Monday. As Bob pointed out, the menu is most extensive. There are many intriguing extras such as homemade bread, lemon butter with cinnamon crackers, and also apple butter. I believe I've covered the main dishes of the menu a number of times in past editions and each time I visit I'm torn between trying something new or sticking to my old favorites. I also find that the Smokehouse and Gift Shop seem to grow between visits.

One of the many joys that I find in preparing each edition of this book is my yearly visit with Walter and Madeline Stoudt at Moselem Springs Inn. It delights me to hear from so many people each year who share my enthusiasm.

MOSELEM SPRINGS INN, P.O. address: R.D. #3, Box 10; Fleetwood, Pa. 19522; 215-944-8212. A historic restaurant restored to 19th century opulence on U.S. 222, at the intersection of Pa. 662, 13 mi. from Reading, and 18 mi. from Allentown. No lodgings. Lunch and dinner. Closed Friday night and all day Saturday. Also Christmas Day. Madeline Stoudt, Innkeeper.

RED ROSE INN, West Grove

"These roses are in bloom from July to October," explained Janice Clanton. They certainly were in bloom on this beautiful August day. There were rolling fields of roses almost as far as the eye could see. We had stepped across Route 796, leaving the warm, red brick building of the Red Rose Inn for a moment to stroll in this truly incredible beauty.

"Here is the living catalog of Star Roses," she said pointing to a planting of about one hundred varieties named in alphabetical order so that the visitor could easily find any variety and see it in bloom before making a purchase.

"Actually, these fields are in bloom before July perhaps even early June, and the blooms go on until the first of October. People come from all over the world. We are just a few minutes away from Longwood Gardens at Kennett Square and another short drive to the Winterthur Gardens over the line in Delaware. Both of them are beautiful." Janice spoke with such enthusiasm that it was infectious.

It was this kind of enthusiasm that brought Janice and Ray Clanton to the Red Rose a number of years ago.

"Oh yes, Ray and I worked here quite a number of years before we decided to buy it. The first thing we did was to restore the cellar in the old 1740 section of the building; I took you down there earlier. It is our antique and gift shop now. Later on we added the William Penn Room and renovated the original, old carriage house into a lounge."

The interior of the inn has been very tastefully furnished with ladder-back chairs, corner cupboards, watercolors and oils. It has exposed brick walls, heavy beams overhead, and also several fireplaces.

Here at the Red Rose, honey baked chicken is a big speciality, but it certainly runs neck and neck with the various mushroom dishes, as this is one of the outstanding sections for the growing of mushrooms, and they are delivered fresh daily to the inn.

As I have mentioned in previous editions, on the first Saturday after Labor Day there is a very touching ceremony re-enacted at the Red Rose Inn depicting the yearly payment of one red rose, paid by a prominent person to a direct descendant of William Penn. He was the original owner of all this land. The ceremony is usually attended by several thousand people. It is the busiest day of the year for the Red Rose Inn.

RED ROSE INN, West Grove, Pa. 19390; 215-869-9964. A country restaurant on Rte. 1, 40 mi. from Philadelphia, near Longwood Gardens and adjacent rose fields. Lunch and dinner served daily, except Tuesday, Fourth of July and New Years Day. Janice and Ray Clanton, Innkeepers.

WHITE ROCK MANOR, Fayetteville

Bob Huffman was telling me about the White Rock Manor's plantation style dinner which is served on Friday, Saturday and Sunday nights. I happened to be there on a Thursday night, and the steak I had eaten was delicious.

"It's a six-course dinner. First we have a condiment tray usually spiced with peaches and crabapples, and served with our homemade nut bread. This is followed by the appetizer tray, and then the salad which is usually crabmeat or shrimp. Then our waiters, working in teams, bring in the soup of the day. It might be egg drop, onion, seafood chowder or corn chowder . . . . all homemade.

"The main courses offered include Spanish chicken with yellow rice, tampas arroz con pollo, or Delmonico steak pan fried with peppers which, by the way, was the hit of the St. Louis Fair." He smiled for a moment and remarked that at White Rock Manor they try to keep pretty much "turn-of-the-century."

"We have a seafood dish which is a sort of crab newburg served in a sherry sauce with a generous portion of scallops and shrimps. Then the dessert tray is rolled in with a choice of cheesecake or one of our plantation sundaes."

There are several reasons to visit the White Rock Manor. The first, I think, has been definitely established as the food. The second would be the building itself, which has a fascinating history going back to the Civil War and includes a visit by the famous Jeb Stuart. It was built as a plantation in 1812. Judith Huffman gives all new guests a wonderful tour which even includes going down into the cellar. The third reason is the beautiful countryside.

The White Rock Manor is just 20 miles from Gettysburg, Pennsylvania, and is adjacent to a golf course which enables the golfers to come in for a snack as they tour the 18 holes.

There is also a very extensive gift shop that is spread out through the hallway, one of the larger rooms and the old kitchen of the inn. Judith has selected some very attractive gifts, antiques and knick-knacks that are usually associated with country living.

There are no lodgings available at this time. However, Bob and Judith assured me that if travelers call in advance, they will direct them to nearby acceptable motel accommodations.

White Rock Manor is a very exceptional country restaurant located in a building that is rich in history and whose appointments reflect a gentleness usually associated with the mid-19th century. I have included explicit directions to it in the italized paragraph that follows. I found it an adventure in good dining, made even more enjoyable by the friendliness of the innkeepers.

WHITE ROCK MANOR, R.D. #2, Fayetteville, Pa. 17222; 717-352-7357. A historic country restaurant 3 mi. off US 30, 10 mi. east of Chambersburg and I-81. From I-81, Exit 6, take US 30 east to the 1st crossroads beyond PA 997. Turn right — the road is unmarked. Go 3 miles. No lodgings. Potluck lunch served daily. Open 7 days a week from Memorial Day to Labor Day. Wed. through Sun. in winter. Dinner by reservation. Closed Christmas Through New Year's. Robert and Judith Hoffman, Innkeepers.

CENTURY INN, Scenery Hill

I've had a lot of fun since the last edition when I first mentioned the French fried asparagus which is served at the Century Inn. Some of my readers wrote and suggested that there was a printing error; others said that they were so intrigued with the idea that they tried it at home themselves with varying results.

I think it is interesting that here is a country inn contained in a building that dates previous to the year 1794. It is the oldest, continuously kept tavern on the famed National Road, and today it has justifiable fame as the home of French fried asparagus! I'm sure Mary Harrington finds it most amusing, and she would quickly add that besides the asparagus there is French fried cauliflower, eggplant, brussel sprouts and even parsley.

Scenery Hill is located in southwestern Pennsylvania at the gateway to some of the most impressive imagination-inspiring scenery in the east. It is a kind of punctuation point in the western development of the United States. In response to the need to connect the east and west by a national transportation system, in 1806 the Congress authorized the National Pike. The section which crossed Pennsylvania began in Cumberland, Maryland, thus earning the title of the Cumberland Road, and ended in Wheeling which at that time was part of Virginia.

"Construction of the road through the mountains and forest wilderness was both costly and tedious," explained Mary. "It took five years to do the first section, and it was estimated that the road between Uniontown and Washington, the road out in front of the inn, cost about $6400 a mile. That was a tremendous amount in those days. Almost immediately the inn began to enjoy the patronage of the great and near-great of the time, including General Lafayette who took refuge here on May 25, 1825 and Andrew Jackson who came by here twice, once on his way to his inauguration as President of the United States."

One of the reasons why guests re-visit the Century Inn is Mary, herself. The inn has numerous evidences of her artistry. She is an expert painter, decorator, refinisher and collector, and she and her late husband, Dr. Gordon Harrington, found a great deal of satisfaction and happiness in keeping an inn and continually adding to their store of knowledge about things historical.

It was Dr. Harrington who explained to me the fascinating history of the Insurrection Flag, which is the only known flag carried during the Whiskey Rebellion of 1794. The famed flag is now in the sitting room of the inn.

Typical of the collection of antiques that the Harringtons put into this handsome old inn is a Chippendale highboy which was brought from Carlisle, Pennsylvania by Conestoga Wagon in the late 18th century. It is in marvelous condition. Oddly enough, the carved shell drawer at the top is upside down.

There are only a few lodging rooms available at this truly ancient hostelry. I have found that it is always advisable to contact the inn in advance to avoid disappointment.

Now, back to the food, before we reluctantly leave Mary and her inn. People in this section of Pennsylvania drive many miles to enjoy her roast turkey, spring chicken, roast stuffed pork chops, baked ham and breaded shrimp. They also favor the sweet potatoes, applesauce, fluffy whipped potatoes, and even the crisp and tender waffles. The desserts include a varying selection of homemade pies, as well as frozen pecan balls with butterscotch sauce and fresh strawberry shortcake.

Doesn't all this wonderful food, served in a delightfully preserved and restored atmosphere, sound wonderful to you? It does to me.

CENTURY INN, Scenery Hill, Pa. 15360; 412-945-6600. A village inn on Rt. 40, 12 mi. east of Washington, 35 mi. south of Pittsburg. Lodgings. Breakfast, lunch, dinner served to travelers. Closed December 20 to Palm Sunday, and July 4. Mrs. Gordon Harrington, Innkeeper.

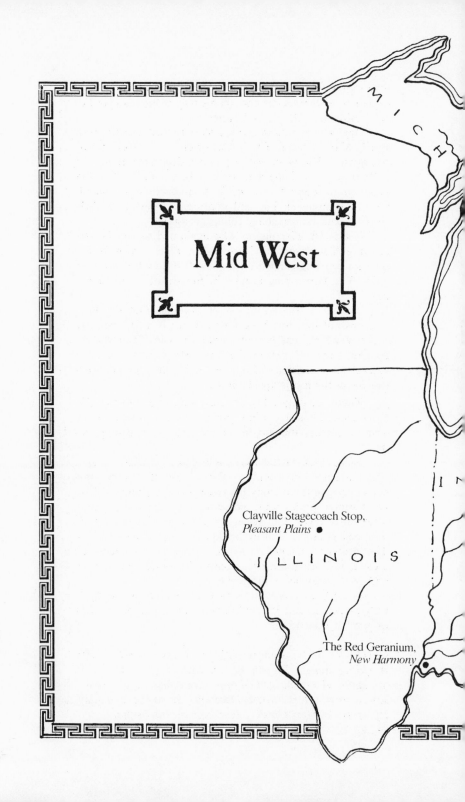

Mid West

M I C H

Clayville Stagecoach Stop,
Pleasant Plains ●

I L L I N O I S

I N

The Red Geranium,
New Harmony ●

Stafford's Bay View Inn,
Petoskey

Leelanau Homestead,
Glen Arbor

St. Clair Inn, *St. Clair*

Botsford Inn, *Farmington*

The Patchwork Quilt,
Middlebury

Welshfield Inn, *Burton*

O H I O

D I A N A

Golden Lamb, *Lebanon*

Ohio

I *crossed the Ohio River on the tiny ferry at Sisters-ville and immediately found myself in a very pleasant, wooded, hilly part of Ohio. State Road #800 passes through Woodsfield, Jerusalem and Barnsville, but there are several unmarked side roads that look most inviting. One of these communities, as I understand, is known as the pumpkin capital of the world. A little to the east, off of Route 148, is an area known as the "Switzerland of Ohio" which according to the scenery is well-named.*

I also did some backroading in the Lebanon area north of Cincinnati, particularly to the west through Mid-dletown and into Richmond, Indiana. Welshfield, which has our second country inn in Ohio, is near Cleveland and there is a real mid-America feel to some of the side roads. At nearby Hiram College I found one of my col-lege roommates. Dr. Paul Rochford, who is head of the Fine Arts Department.

GOLDEN LAMB, Lebanon

As much as I wanted to, I was unable to visit the Golden Lamb during the past Christmas holidays. This remarkable village inn in the heartland of Ohio indeed knows how, as Dickens said, "to keep Christmas well." However, with the aid of my friends Janet and Duke Pinkham, without some mention of whom these editions would be almost incomplete, I'm able to pass on the facts of what has now become a traditional holiday celebration.

As Janet says, "Well, first of all there are the decora-tions. Jack Reynolds must spend days standing on step-ladders hanging the garlands and the wreaths, Christmas bells and the ornaments. The night that Duke and I went for dinner, there was a crackling fire, and the little an-tique music box played traditional Christmas tunes. All of the guest rooms had different decorations on the doors.

"They start Christmas on the first of December, fully decorated, and on the fourth of December they display a group of very early Christmas tree ornaments from a private collection. Chef Erwin Pfiel had 'Frohe Weihnachten' which is a native German meal with roast venison, smoked lox and a Black Forest yule log.

"For a few days in the middle of December they also had a display of antique banks, and the special menu that included a wassail bowl, braised goose and a plum pudding. That's the week that the Christmas caroling starts. There are Christmas carols on the village green and all kinds of activity at the Warren County Historical Museum during the holidays as well.

"Then, for the week before Christmas there is a collection of seasonal ceramic creations by Mrs. Donald Shuttlemeier, and the accompanying menu speciality was called, 'Home For Christmas' which included roast turkey, Smithfield ham, fruit cake and all the trimmings."

Janet also explained that there were other special events, including a holiday buffet of many lands and a "Holiday Happenings" art show. There were many, many more things to make this continually changing pageant of the holidays really outstanding.

A display of original paintings created especially for the Golden Lamb depicts Christmasses at the inn in the past. These original paintings have been made into the Golden Lamb Christmas cards during recent years. The most recent was done by Nancy Simpson.

Christmas season at the Golden Lamb — I certainly won't miss it next year.

GOLDEN LAMB INN, 27 S. Broadway, Lebanon, Ohio 45036; 513-932-5065. A village inn in the heart of Ohio's farming country on US Hwy. 63, 42 and 48; 5 mi. east of **I-75; 3 mi. west of** *I-71. Lodgings. Sunday Breakfast. Lunch and dinner served daily except Christmas. Jackson Reynolds, Innkeeper.*

WELSHFIELD INN, Burton

I reached into my pocket and pulled out a five cent piece, dropped it in the slot, heard it clink and clank its way through some mysterious mechanism, and then suddenly the machine started to play. I recognized the tune immediately, "Barney Google." It was, to say the least, a triumph for my memory of trivia as I sang along with it: "Barney Google, with the goo, goo, googlie eyes; Barney Google with a wife three times his size."

Brian Holmes chuckled, "You'd be surprised how many people know the words." We were standing in the dining room of the Welshfield Inn in Burton, Ohio, and I felt almost as if a newsboy would come in momentarily with the tidings of Dewey's victory at Manila Bay! Here was a part of mid-America at its nostalgic best, and only 25 miles from Cleveland.

Brian and Polly Holmes have as neat and fetching a country inn as I have seen anywhere. Furthermore, the inn has a rather interesting history. It was built, so Brian told me, in the 1840's and was originally known as the Nash Hotel. This was the center part of the building. The front addition was made by a later owner named Dr. Foster, and the name was changed to the Troy Hotel. The proprietor at that time was also the village postmaster. Once again, I've discovered an inn that, during the American un-Civil War, was used as an underground station where slaves were cared for on their escape to Canada.

Polly explained that during the 19th century social affairs were held at the Nash, including spelling matches, a singing school and a dancing school. A ballroom was added under Captain Marcy, as well as several other alterations.

My visits to inns always include an extended stay in the kitchen, and I have seldom seen such a well-organized and executed food-preparing and serving area as at the Welshfield. As Brian explained: "This type of thinking allows time to be spent on such things as preparing the arrangement of food on the plate, about which I'm most particular." It also provides opportunity to do other special things such as homemade preserves, pickles, soups — including a New England clam chowder, which is as tasty as I have ever had.

As usual, I could go on at considerable length about the menu, but sufficeth at this time to say that features such as the fresh country-fried chicken, which is done in an old-fashioned iron skillet and then put in the roaster, makes eating a pleasure. More about all of this next time.

Then, there is that crazy nickelodeon which makes sounds like a piano, violin, mandolin, and flute. That alone would be worth a trip half way across the country. I'm glad I made it.

WELSHFIELD INN, Rte 422, Burton, Ohio 44021; 216-834-4164. A country restaurant on Rte. 422, 25 mi. from Cleveland. Near the Sea World. No lodgings. Lunch and dinner served daily, except Monday. Closed Memorial Day,, July 2-5, Sept. 4, Nov. 23-Dec. 24, and first 4 weeks in January. Brian and Polly Holmes, Innkeepers.

Indiana

New Harmony — the name alone says much about the hopes and inspirations of two separate groups of early 19th century settlers. The first in 1814 were from Wurtenberg, Germany who prospered under the leadership of George Rapp. They were dissenters from the German Lutheran Church, and like the Shakers, practiced celibacy which they considered to be a desirable condition consistant with their purpose to live like the early Christians.

In 1824, a group under the leadership of Robert Owen, a Welsh social reformer, purchased the community from the earlier Harmonists. Their purpose was to create "a universal happiness through universal education." They chose to establish their community in America where expression of thought was free. These people succeeded in attracting scientists and educators both from Europe and the United States to New Harmony.

Their achievements at New Harmony include the establishment of the first free public school system in America, the first free library, the first kindergarten, the first trade school, the first women's club with a written constitution and the first civic drama club. It was also the seat of the first geological survey in the United States.

Of great importance is the fact that in 1834 girls and boys in New Harmony had equal access to education.

In the next edition of this book we'll have a closer look at the effect of these two communal movements on life in the United States. The important thing now is to point out that a great many of the buildings from the early part of the 19th century have been carefully preserved and restored. Of more recent vintage, however, is that the Paul Tillich Park has been laid out. Everyone of all faiths is invited to enter the Roofless Church, the focal point of which is Jacques Lipchitz' sculpture "Descent of the Holy Spirit."

I found that there is much of great uplift and value to be found in New Harmony.

RED GERANIUM, New Harmony

I well remember the day I first visited the Red Geranium. It was warm and sunny and although I had missed the full blooming of the Golden Rain Trees which takes place in late June, there were still vestiges of this wondrous event visible to give a clue to the beauty.

With Mary Ellen Gerard as an attractive guide, I discovered that the inn consists of a combination of different types of buildings, all beautifully landscaped, located just a few steps from the side entrance to the Roofless Church and immediately in front of Paul Tillich Park.

An early indication that this would be something unusual was the menu. It was printed in four delicate natural colors with a very handsome blue cover on which is embossed a bright red geranium blossom. It has many pages of imaginative prose about highly imaginative food.

The first thing that Innkeeper Gary Gerard said that I must try was the fresh spinach salad. "A local lady grows it for us especially," he said. "But, we are very fortunate as there is a long growing season here and vegetables are readily available. We have fresh corn on the cob on July 1st!" I poured some special Red Gera-

New Harmony street scene

nium French dressing on the salad and my first bite made me a believer.

This was accompanied by the hottest homemade bread I'd ever eaten. The butter melted on it instantly. Incidentally, there is a bake shop connected with the inn where all of the homemade goodies are on sale.

I cite the main dish that particular noon as an example of the Red Geranium's originality. It was char-prime steak. Mary Ellen explained that the whole prime rib is cooked rare in the oven and then sliced and put on the grill for the last few minutes. My slice was a half inch thick, and I most certainly did sop up the gravy with that delicious bread!

For dessert that day I had a small piece of two different types of pies. The first was lemon Shaker and the second was fresh strawberry.

The tour of the inn after lunch with Gary and Mary Ellen consisted of one fascinating feature after another. For example, there is a beautiful, little private dining room with a two-story vaulted ceiling that is completely covered with pastoral paintings.

The newest dining room has glass on one whole side which gives it an al fresco feeling. The view is of Tillich Park, the orchards, cornfields, the grass, and the trees.

Throughout the inn there is a strong feeling of continuous creativity and this is personified by the cast iron figures on the white fireplace in the main dining room sculptured by Mary Calvery called "Sons of the Morning." It is six or seven feet long and shows young people involved in play activity.

There is much more to say about New Harmony, Indiana and the Red Geranium. It is a rewarding blend of past and present, with an outstanding country restaurant to bring the two together. One of the most fulfilling rewards for writing a book like this, is the opportunity it affords to encourage our readers to discover more for themselves.

RED GERANIUM, New Harmony, Ind. 47631; 812-682-4431. A country restaurant in a historically famous town on Rte. 460, 20 mi. west of Evansville. No lodgings for 1973. Lunch and dinner served every day except Monday and Christmas Day. Gary Gerard, Innkeeper.

PATCHWORK QUILT, Middlebury

The man on duty at Exit 10 of the Indiana Turnpike responded quickly and with good humor to my inquiry regarding the location of the Patchwork Quilt. "Turn left at the end of the access road and then turn left at the first road on the left. Just follow it around."

This is what I was doing, and the sunset here in the heartland of mid-America was almost beyond description. There were great streaks of red in the western skies. The road threads its way between Milton's and Arletta's acres and then up to the very doorway of the Patchwork Quilt.

As I saw the hay rakes and farm machinery, it occurred to me that this might be the only time many people traveling who live in large cities would have the opportunity to see something of a working farm. I wandered among the barns where there were chickens and

Indiana farmland

pigs, and because there were great cornfields on all sides, there was a collection of corn cribs. For indeed, this is a farm restaurant.

I find many of the hallmarks for which I search in country inns here at the Patchwork Quilt. For example, there is the "nosewarmer," a non-alcoholic drink which greets everyone. It might be a hot mulled cider or cranberry juice. There is also a blackboard which notes the names and home towns of the guests who will be dining that evening.

The kitchen is such a showplace with its many stoves and ovens, that I always walk through on the way to the dining room. Here, everyone is given a bowl of steaming homemade soup, frequently bubbling away in a large iron pot on the hearth.

Then the appetizers are served buffet style. I counted over thirty on my last visit.

A lot of us probably didn't have grandmothers that lived on farms, but if she had, she might have served baked ham or a special chicken or one of the dozens of other outstanding dishes featured from time to time on the menu. I will say this, that grandmother's rolls were never like Arletta's.

And it's for certain that grandmother never had such a selection of delicious desserts. These include fantastic looking (and tasting) cakes, pies, tortes and other goodies, and they are all homemade.

The only meal served at the Patchwork Quilt is dinner, and it is always necessary to reserve in advance. I've had many people write me and say how disappointed they were that they failed to remember this. Dinner is not served at all on Sunday.

My stay at the Patchwork Quilt is always an adventure in eating. It is the next best thing to living on a farm!

PATCHWORK QUILT COUNTRY INN, R.R. #2, Box 241, Middlebury, Ind. 46450; 219-825-2417. Interchange #10 on the Indiana Toll Rd. A working farm restaurant in the tradition of mid-western hospitality. Dinner served daily by reservation. Closed Sunday and Christmas. Milton and Arletta Lovejoy, Innkeepers.

Illinois

CLAYVILLE STAGECOACH STOP, Pleasant Plains

Dr. Emmet Pearson and I were standing in front of the old fireplace with it's bread baking oven and utensils from the last century. He picked up the large iron skillet and tapped on it with his finger, as if for emphasis.

"I hope that we've creat-ed an environment here," he said. "We're trying to both preserve and restore the life of early Illinois.

Old fireplace and oven

"We started with this building, which was the Broadwell Tavern, and was one of the first brick build-ings to be constructed in this part of the country. It was built by two brothers named Broadwell around 1824. The community was named for the Whig presidential candi-date, Henry Clay. Incidental-ly, Abraham Lincoln was the lawyer for the Broadwells for a period of twenty years and actually tried two cases before the Supreme Court for them.

"Mrs. Pearson and I entered the picture a few years ago when we saw what remained of this building and have painstakingly restored the tavern to what we hope is close to its true status of about 140 years ago. The architecture is called Federal, a simple American style ideally adapted for the frontier where skilled workmen were quite scarce.

"However, in recent years we have reached out from the restoration of the Tavern to try to assemble artifacts, tools and implements used on Illinois farms and preserve them in the Farmer's Museum. We also have a pottery studio, a barn theatre, and a pioneer craft shop showing gardening, spinning, pottery, candlemaking and black-smithing."

To provide food for the many visitors, the Pearsons have asked the local farm ladies to run the Clayville Country Kitchen which utilizes as much of the local farm produce as possible. They call upon the talents of the local farm folk for delicious pies, cakes and individual dishes.

It is open for lunch and light dinners daily, except Monday. There are no guest lodgings.

The Clayville Stagecoach Stop is a successful combination of many efforts in restoring and preserving some of the best of the American past. It is quite near New Salem, a restored village where Abraham Lincoln met and courted Ann Rutledge. Visiting Broadwell's Tavern, observing the many old country crafts which are being taught, and enjoying the country food much the same as it was in the mid-nineteenth century, is a notable experience. Of particular interest is the Annual Crafts Festival which takes place on the next to the last Friday and Saturday in October.

CLAYVILLE STAGECOACH STOP, (1834), Pleasant Plains, Ill. 62677; 217-626-3651. A restored community on Rte. 125, 12 mi. west of Springfield. Among the features are Broadwell's Tavern, restored to it's original 1834 condition and the Clayville Country Kitchen. Clayville has recently been donated to Sangamond State University of Springfield, which has an enthusiastic program for expansion, development, teaching and entertainment. Open lodgings available.

Michigan

Again I find myself indebted to Jim Mellow. This time for pointing out some of the beauties of Michigan. Although we had never seen one another, I arranged to meet him at 12 noon at Gwen Frostic's Studio near Benzonia. We each carried a copy of "Country Inns and Back Roads" in order to identify the other. It was a most happy meeting for me because later the entire Mellow family came to Stockbridge and we all enjoyed dinner together, and I am planning on seeing them again in Michigan this summer. With Jim's help, I discovered Frankfort, Crystal Lake, Beulah, and the surrounding communities which are a very pleasant vacation area. The visit to the Frostic Studio was an experience in itself, and it was most enlightening to see how some of this remarkable woman's great designs are created and reproduced.

On this trip, I did have a wonderful dinner with my good friends, Clare and Lucy Dee Dee. They have visited here in Stockbridge and have been most helpful in finding new inns.

Leelanau County, and the areas around Glen Lake resemble parts of New England. One of the most rewarding back roads is Route 131 from Petoskey, around Little Traverse Bay, and up to Cross Village. In a great many places, the road runs right along the shores of Lake Michigan.

Bay View library

STAFFORD'S BAY VIEW INN, Petoskey

Stafford Smith and I were talking and rocking on the Victorian porch of this 80-year-old inn, with an eye on Little Traverse Bay where we could watch the water skiing and sailboats. I asked him about Bay View.

"The Bay View section of Petoskey is a summer religious, music, and art center. It is quite similar to Oak Bluff on Martha's Vineyard in Massachusetts. It was organized in the last quarter of the 19th century.

147

Bay View flourished during the height of the time that northern Michigan became a summer resort," explained Stafford. "In those days people came from Detroit, Chicago, Cleveland, and even the east to spend the whole summer in Bay View. That was when they built those Victorian cottages. The cultural and religious programs which started then are still going on now and provide a wonderful atmosphere for a summer vacation. Of course, our inn is a direct extension of all of that, and we are located right on the edge of Bay View."

This was my second trip to this lovely section of northern Michigan. Nancy and I had visited there the previous year, and were immediately impressed with Stafford and Janice Smith and the energy and dedication that they put into this beautiful inn.

I mentioned in a previous edition how one of the outstanding features is the fact that older people are made to feel most welcome. It is a sort of meeting place for grandparents and children. "I think that's easily explained," said Janice, as she joined us for a moment. "There are all kinds of summer water sports, and tennis, and hiking for younger people, and there is golf and all of the programs in Bay View to interest more mature people. Everybody can have a good time."

They make a very attractive couple, Stafford and Janice. They met here in the inn in 1960 when Stafford was the assistant manager and Janice was the hostess. Then they purchased the inn and were married in 1961, and since that time they have completely redecorated and refurnished it. There is a great deal of emphasis on good food.

"Yes, we always wanted to keep a friendly inn, such as the kind that one usually associates with New England," explained Stafford. "Our cousins have the country inn in Chocorua, New Hampshire."

Well, the inn has grown in many ways since 1961, and now because of the skiing activity in the area, it remains open during Christmas week and every weekend during ski season.

The more I travel, the more I think that inns like the Bay View Inn and areas like Petoskey, where at one time the guests spent luxurious long summer days reading, talking and relishing a leisurely living place, are again coming into their own.

STAFFORD'S BAY VIEW INN, Box 3, Petoskey, Mich. 49770; 616-347-2771. A resort inn on Little Traverse Bay in the Bay View section of Petoskey. Mod. American Plan and European Plan. Breakfast, lunch and dinner served to travelers June to Sept. Open 3rd week in June until week after Labor Day. Open Christmas week and weekends during snow season. Alpine and xc ski. Stafford and Janice Smith, Innkeepers.

LEELANAU HOMESTEAD, Glen Harbor

There we were back in January, first month of the year. What an appropriate time to be talking over dinner about a new baby . . . well, a new 1929 baby. Dick Huey and Jim Stephen, his business partner, call it the "rebirth of a country inn."

We were talking about The Leelanau Homestead, a resort with a 44-year history located 250 miles north of Detroit on the shores of Lake Michigan. Dick and Jim told me their exciting plans.

These include a brand new entrance to be completed this spring through the hardwood hills to the east. This new entrance terminates at the old Center, now completely remodeled and rechristened Homestead Reception Center.

"Here you will register on arrival," said Dick. "Later it will be a place to relax on the big brown leather couches in front of a roaring fire in the fieldstone fireplace. Outside, you can lounge on the overlook deck, with panoramic views of Sleeping Bear Bay, the dunes, and the Manitou Islands."

Dick continued: "From the Reception Center will be a re-graded, re-landscaped Homestead Road to the original Homestead building, now called The Inn at the Homestead. Its familiar exterior, stripped of the addi-

Winter scene

tions to the building and windows redone, hides a spanking new kitchen and completely rebuilt, redecorated candlelight dining rooms.

"The view will include an entirely new jetty and walkway system along the Crystal River, with a complete low voltage lighting system that makes it sparkle softly after dark. The walkway lighting extends the length of the grounds in keeping with a new emphasis on evening activities. To the north, in Oak Ridge, both tennis courts will be rebuilt from the ground up, and a third, lighted, court will be in place."

The Inn itself is the heart of a 200-acre parcel right in the center of the Sleeping Bear Dunes National Lakeshore. Dick and Jim emphasized that the beautiful shore of the lake, the precious sand dunes, the river's edge, and the steep forested slopes behind the Homestead will also be preserved permanently even on the Homestead's property.

I first visited The Leelanau Homestead a number of years ago, and it was for me a totally delightful experience. The things that Dick and Jim are now planning will continue to enhance this experience and add a great many new dimensions. The grand opening of the "new" old Inn at the Homestead is set for sometime in June. I'll be visiting there in the middle of the summer and from what I have seen already, it will be a unique experience.

THE LEELANAU HOMESTEAD, Glen Arbor, Mich. 49636; 616-334-3041 (In Michigan 800-632-1708). A complete resort inn on M22, 30 mi. from Traverse City. Located in northwestern Michigan on the shore of Lake Michigan. Lodgings. Breakfast, lunch, dinner served to travelers daily. Alpine and xc ski. Dick Huey and Jim Stephen, Innkeepers.

THE BOTSFORD INN, Farmington

"You know, I used to hate to come to Detroit." My newly-acquired acquaintance was obviously warming to his subject. "I used to get into one of those big hotels downtown and spend the night looking at the T.V. I'm a sort of family man, and I don't go out on the town if my wife isn't along. So, what else is there to do?" I nodded, in complete agreement.

Model T Ford

"Then my wife picked up a book at our bookstore about country inns . . . . ."

At this point my stomach, which was gratefully filled with Botsford Inn roast beef and other choice goodies, began to have a sinking sensation. What next, I thought.

"One night when I was home, she was reading it and called out: "Harry, do you realize that there is a country inn in Detroit?"

"Well, to make a long story short, we read about how the Botsford was started about 135 years ago as a stagecoach stop and how Henry Ford became interested in it in 1924 and put many of his own antiques and treasures in it as well. That part about the garden, the swimming pool, the green grass and the tall trees convinced me that I ought to stop here the next time."

"Anyway, that's how I happen to be here. This is about my sixth time. Now I know John Anhut, the innkeeper, the waitresses, the people out at the front desk, and it is sort of home away from home. I never thought that there would be a place like this near a big, impersonal city where I could come in, maybe take a swim, meet a couple of other salesmen, talk shop, and have dinner with them; then after a nice, pleasant evening, go to a quiet bedroom and wake up in the morning and see the trees and hear the birds!

"And look at the antiques they've got here. I understand there has been an inn here since early in the 19th century. I think Mr. Ford restored it back in the '20's."

I was now beginning to feel very secure.

"I'll tell you something else. The last time I came here I brought my two little boys and my wife, and they toured Greenfield Village while I did my business. The people at the front desk told me about the St. Clair Inn up on the river north of Detroit, so we went up there for a day and had a wonderful time. I sure would like to meet the man who wrote that book."

I put out my hand.

BOTSFORD INN, 2800 Grand River, Farmington, Mich. 48024;313-KE7-4200. A village inn on the city line of Detroit. Lodgings. Breakfast and lunch served daily except Monday. Dinner served daily. John Anhut, Innkeeper.

ST. CLAIR INN, St. Clair

The Dutch doors on my little guest house at the St. Clair Inn looked out on the green lawn that led to the river's edge. Just a few steps away on the rustic walk, Creighton Holden had placed one of the largest birdhouses I had ever seen — a veritable feathered condominium. What a warbling and chirping ensued!

The evening of my arrival had been slightly foggy and I became instantly aware of the whistles. I heard deep-throated demands and responses pitched from E flat to C natural. The polyphony lulled me to sleep! As the ore boats passed within hailing distance of the inn's boardwalk, the fog obscured the form of their super-structure so that they looked like the final act of the Flying Dutchman.

Fortunately, the morning was clear and bright and the river sparkled in the sun. I stood for a while on the terrace before going in to breakfast, admiring the red brick and half-timbered Tudor architecture which has had a few additions over recent years.

I felt miles away from Detroit, and yet the ride out

had taken a little more than a half hour. This morning there were some new cruisers moored at the inn's dock, and I could see one gentleman with his golf bag leave the dock area and head up to the inn. He was, no doubt, planning to play 18 this afternoon at the St. Clair Country Club.

There is a story of St. Clair, the town that should be an inspiration for all communities that seemed to be dying, whose spirit is not crushed, but whose buildings, streets and appearances are inadequate to meet modern demands. St. Clair was in this position as recently as 1961. The stores, with their outmoded fronts, were being vacated. Retail business was going elsewhere, and the young people were leaving town in ever-increasing numbers. Worst of all, the waterfront, once the pride of the community, was a shambles.

However, a spark was ignited, and the local businessmen and civic leaders put their heads together in some painful self-evaluation sessions, many held in the St. Clair Inn. Out of these original conferences came planning and coordination with Federal funds and new designs and objectives. Today, the business section of St. Clair stands as a monument to perserverance and patience.

The St. Clair Inn has maintained a steady reputation over the years for good food and comfortable lodgings. The latter is in wide variety. Rooms in the main building of the inn are homelike and comfortable, and the small suites are a bit more elaborate. The interior is Scottish baronial, with massive furniture, deep chairs and couches, and rich Highland tartans. The little touches include warm bread, fresh from the oven, hot potato soup with onions which is served with warm crackers.

The St. Clair Inn, known as "The Inn on the River" has been a landmark since the mid-1920's. There are beautiful homes along the river at this point, with lawns that extend to the water's edge. The inn fits right in.

ST. CLAIR INN, St. Clair, Mich. 48079; 313-329-2222. A river inn with many resort features, 50 mi. north of Detroit on the shores of the St. Clair River via I-94. Well known for the Great Lakes water traffic passing directly in front. Lodgings. Breakfast, lunch, dinner served daily except Christmas. Creighton Holden, Innkeeper.

South

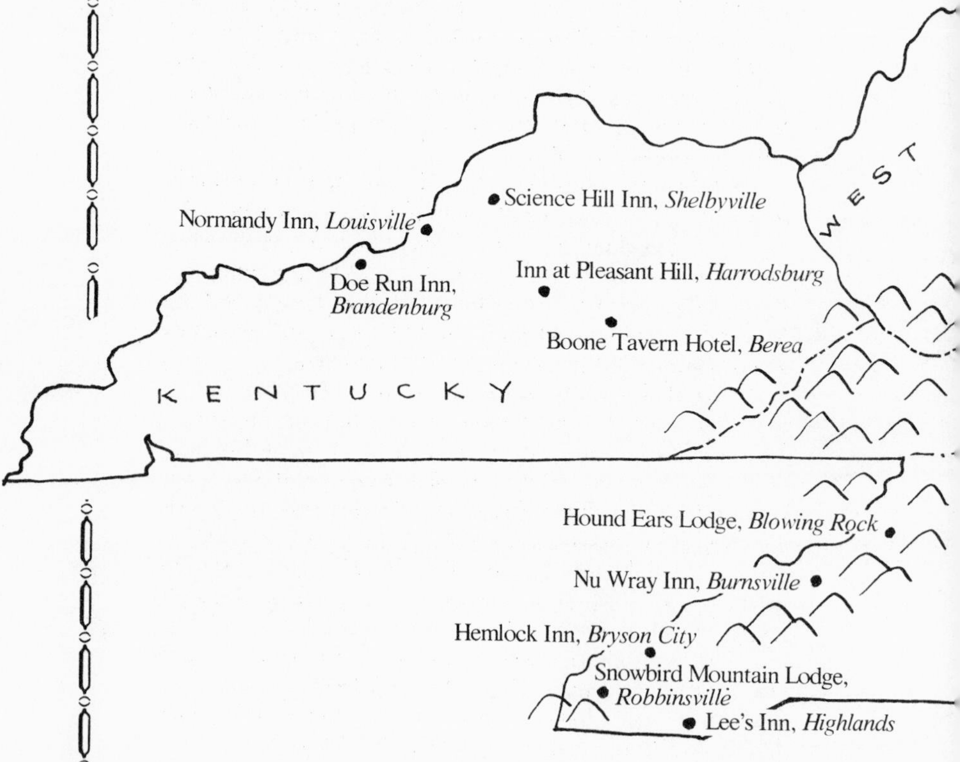

Normandy Inn, *Louisville* •

• Science Hill Inn, *Shelbyville*

Doe Run Inn,
Brandenburg •

Inn at Pleasant Hill, *Harrodsburg*
•

Boone Tavern Hotel, *Berea* •

WEST

K E N T U C K Y

Hound Ears Lodge, *Blowing Rock* •

Nu Wray Inn, *Burnsville* •

Hemlock Inn, *Bryson City* •

Snowbird Mountain Lodge,
• *Robbinsville*

• Lee's Inn, *Highlands*

Drovers Inn, *Wellsburg*

Wells Inn, *Sistersville*

Park View Inn, *Berkeley Springs*

Wayside Inn, *Middletown*

Maryland Inn, *Annapolis*

Old Club Restaurant, *Alexandria*

Robert Morris Inn, *Oxford*

MARYLAND

VIRGINIA

Faraway Hills, *Beverly*

Graves Mountain Lodge, *Syria*

General Lewis Inn, *Lewisburg*

Lakeview Lodge, *Roanoke*

VIRGINIA

Colonial Inn, *Hillsborough*

NORTH

CAROLINA

Maryland

Although it has a relatively small area, Maryland extends from the Antlantic Ocean to the Allegheny Mountains. The one dominant feature is the Chesapeake Bay. For some years, we have been rewarded by our yearly visit to Maryland's Eastern Shore where the inn at Oxford is on the eastern shore of the Bay. It makes an interesting contrast to a village inn in Annapolis that was established in 1772 or thereabouts.

ROBERT MORRIS INN, Oxford

The postcard was dated June 16th. It was from my friend, Captain Bill Benson, the man who operates the ferry between Oxford and Bellevue, Maryland. It said, in part, "Thank you very much for the autographed copy of 'Country Inns and Back Roads'. I hope to see you soon again."

Reading this card, which had a drawing of the ferry by John Moll, took me back to the conversation I had with Captain Benson as we made our way across the three quarters of a mile wide Tred Avon River. As we talked, the Mansard roof of the Robert Morris Inn loomed larger and larger. I had strolled from the inn down to the dock to say "hello" to him, and we started talking about early Oxford and the Chesapeake Bay area and the marvelous east coast of Maryland. So I stayed on for a ride to the other side, and after we had disembarked the two automobiles, he noticed the square white board used for a signal back on the Robert Morris side — so we were going back empty. That didn't seem to bother him.

Captain Bill's ferry, upon which have ridden the great and near great, as well as the humble, is just one of the many unique attractions about Oxford, which is one of the oldest towns in Maryland. Even to this day it manages to maintain its colonial charm. It is a perfect setting for an inn of such integrity and antiquity as the Robert Morris. The antiquity dates to the early 18th century.

Earlier in the afternoon I was up on the third floor with Innkeeper Ken Gibson and his wife Wendy, looking at the unbelievably high, beautiful four-poster bed. In fact, it was so high that it was necessary to have a set of stairs to climb into it. (There is also one at the Island House in Ogunquit, Maine.) Underneath there was a trundle bed. When I asked Ken whether it was much in demand for honeymoons, he explained that it was, even though that particular room had no private bathroom.

"Most of the others do," said Wendy, "however, this is a great curiousity and it is the subject of a lot of good natured kidding."

In the four or more trips that I have made to the Robert Morris, I found that they aren't kidding about the idea of providing excellent food and accommodations to the many visitors who come to the Eastern shore every year. To this end, an entire new kitchen was installed last year and is a model for cleanliness and organization.

Captain Bill Benson's Oxford-Bellevue ferry

Whereas, I find these things fascinating, I must say that I am even more intrigued by the array of Maryland cooking that features forth from it everyday! These include Maryland crab in many sundry mutations, baked rockfish stuffed with crabmeat, fried clams, crab soup with pieces of back fin, crab Imperial and stuffed soft shell crabs. There are also hot, homemade breads, and desserts include strawberry pie with whipped cream, slightly tart and a delicious mocha cake.

Gosh, I wish I was back on Captain Bill Benson's ferry headed for the Robert Morris at dinnertime, right now!

By the way, Ken and Wendy Gibson are enthusiastic travelers, and during a trip last year stayed at several of the inns mentioned in this book, sending back glowing accounts of their holiday. Along with Todd and Penny Drucquer, at the Pump House Inn in Cavadensis, Pa., they are two of the youngest innkeepers we've met.

ROBERT MORRIS INN, Oxford, Md. 21654; 301-226-5111. A village inn in a secluded Colonial community on the banks of the Tred Avon, about 1½ hrs. from Washington via the Bay Bridge. Lodgings. Continental breakfast, lunch and dinner served daily except Monday. Open year round, closed Christmas Day. Kenneth Gibson, Innkeeper.

MARYLAND INN, Annapolis

My choice of rooms at the Maryland Inn? . . . . I paused between the intimate rooms where the building is just one room wide, overlooking rooftops of the Colonial town, and those giving a glimpse down Church Street to the 18th Century waterfront.

White sails sparkling on a blue-sky Bay invite me to bring my family for a sailing vacation. Or, to share a feeling of the working watermen, on the fleet of Skipjacks or Bug-eyes, who bring in the day's "drudge" of oysters.

I am visiting Annapolis, a town whose vivid history I value, because of the things it teaches us about our past.

In the 1770's when the Maryland Inn was built, the Innkeeper or Ordinarykeeper, as he was called, was required to provide stabling for at least ten horses plus a store of oats and hay. Though hitching posts no longer flank the front entrance, the inn retains that refreshing warmth and strong spirit which characterized the Colonial period.

Thomas Hyde built the Inn, and advertised it as "an elegant Brick house in a dry and healthy part of the city . . .one of the first houses in the state for a house of entertainment." What entertainment Hyde had in mind nobody knows, but today a guest can participate in one of the Inn's annual holiday celebrations: Bastille Day (July 14), Heritage Weekend (Mid-October), Thanksgiving, Christmas and New Year's Eve (when there is roast goose and a Minstrel). Darting Tournaments, and Dominoes. . . all traditional in English Pubs, are popular afternoon and evening in the Drummer's Lot. Or, one can enjoy the restored King of France Tavern, where the old stone walls form a fitting backdrop for the talents of such important names in the history of American music as Teddy Wilson, Earl "Fatha" Hines, and guitarist, Charlie Byrd.

I enjoyed dinner in the Ordinary. The brick-walled dining room, with its original fireplaces, provides the best in Chesapeake Bay seafoods. Two specialties: hot corn sticks and cream of crab soup are exceptional. A smattering of European foods: escargots, Quiche Lorraine, steak au Poivre, oysters a la Gino, provide an unexpected pleasure.

We settled into the loveseat by the fire after dinner to collect our impressions of the town created by the guide from Historic Annapolis earlier in the day. Stories of Madison, Jefferson, Franklin and the handsome Marquis de Lafeyette; and of George and Martha Wash-

Annapolis street scene

159

ington who often journeyed from Mount Vernon to attend the horse races. The great houses of the distinguished men of that day are still here—Charles Carroll of Carrollton, Governor William Paca, Horatio Sharpe, Ridout, Middleton and Reynolds.

Here within a few paces of the inn, is the State House with its graceful dome, where the legislature meets annually to argue bills, much as they did 200 years ago.

It is rewarding to find a town *and* an Inn whose blend of old and new is so successful in providing the warmth and comfort of another era.

MARYLAND INN, Church Circle, Annapolis, Md. 21401; 301-263-2641. An 18th century inn in a history-laden town. Near the U.S. Naval Academy and Chesapeake Bay. Lodgings. European Plan. Breakfast, lunch, dinner served daily. Anne Pearson May, Innkeeper.

Virginia

Virginia has one of the great back roads of all times — the Skyline Drive, which runs from Front Royal southwest to Roanoke and then goes into the Blue Ridge Parkway into the Carolinas. It is completly free of any signs or commercial establishments, although there are restaurants and waystations that are maintained by the state. It abounds in overlooks and wayside markers. It is crisscrossed by east-west roads along its entire length, so that it is possible to leave at many different points to return to the rude world if you wish. There are no guard rails on this narrow road, and the posted speed limits are wisely set. Running parallel to it on the western slopes of the Blue Ridge is I-81, which provides fast transportation but isn't all that exciting in places. However, the old road, US 11, runs down the Shenandoah Valley and is a little closer to what Virginia is all about today, with towns like Waynesboro, Steel's Tavern, Lexington and Harrisonburg.

Although at the moment I have not found any inns on Virginia's Northern Neck, this is a most historically oriented area and comes under the influence of the Chesapeake Bay. You're apt to find that your back road ends as a dead end against a creek that has no bridge.

Mt. Vernon, home of George Washington

OLD CLUB RESTAURANT, Alexandria

"The food must be good," I thought, "because the natives eat here."

In this case, the "natives" whose cars were in the Old Club's parking lot, were the business people of Alexandria and nearby Washington. I look at the license plates with interest, and at times learn a lot.

I stopped long enough to look at the very well-kept grounds. I was looking, in particular, for the English walnut tree and the black walnut tree that are said to have been given to General Washington by the Marquis de Lafayette. Although we were just a few squares from downtown Alexandria, the white fence and high hedges provided an attractive cushion against the urban intrusions. I particularly liked the terrace with lush grass growing between the flagstones.

The last time I stopped here with my son Keith, and we both enjoyed the Virginia country ham served over cornbread and covered with maple syrup. This time, however, I resisted this in favor of Allegheny mountain trout, which was baked boneless and stuffed with mushrooms and rice. A good tartar sauce was the topper. We might have ordered chicken Laura Lee, which is a chicken breast on hickory ham with a mushroom sauce. Both of these are really something!

The oldest part of this colonial house was built by George Washington and his friends as a private club. The little brick building on the north is said to have been young Washington's office while he was surveying this area. There are dozens of little stories connected with this place, including the fact that during the War of 1812 when the enemy was at the gates of Alexandria, all the good furniture was buried in the vegetable garden. I hope none of it got mixed-up with the carrots and peas!

Speaking of my son, Keith, this was for him as it is for so many people from the north, the first time that he had ever visited a restaurant where real southern food was served. One of the things that he simply couldn't resist was the peanut soup which is a feature at the Old Club. I am very fond of it myself, although as a result of visiting this historic restaurant many times over the years, have learned that a cup of it will be just perfect, rather than a bowl.

On that visit Keith and I drove down the George Washington Parkway and parked at a very convenient distance so that we spent part of the afternoon at the Washington Monument and the Lincoln Memorial. They are both just a few pleasant moments from Alexandria.

As we looked at the picture of George and Martha Washington hung over the beautiful fireplace in the Club Room, Jack said, "Now you're a member of George Washington's club."

OLD CLUB RESTAURANT, 555 So. Washington St., Alexandria, Va. 22314; 703-KI 9-4555. Just across the river from Washington, D.C. in one of the country's best preserved Colonial cities. Lunch and dinner served daily, except Mondays and Christmas. No lodgings available. John Coleman, Innkeeper.

WAYSIDE INN, Middletown

Innkeeper Herb White and I were standing in the new Senseney Room of the Wayside Inn admiring the 40-foot mural depicting the battle of Cedar Creek.

"It was on November 12, 1864," he said, "that the Southern forces under Jubal Early put the Union forces to flight." He pointed to a building in the picture and said: "That is the Wayside Inn at that time. By the way, this room is named for the original founder of Middletown, Dr. Peter Senseney."

The Wayside Inn dates from at least 1797. It is correctly referred to as an historic restoration. It was thoughtfully restored to its present form in 1960 when Leo Bernstein, lawyer and banker from nearby Washington, happened to drive down the main street in Middletown and saw the inn's tremendous possibilities.

Since that time, he has filled all of the inn lodging rooms and public rooms with

Belle Grove Mansion

a remarkable group of antiques from his private collection. Many of them are from the Colonial period. The new Senseney Room is furnished with a great many exceptional pieces.

In the past, I have always enjoyed taking dinner in The Slave Kitchen. He showed me another little hideaway dining room with brick flooring and an almost Old World feeling. Also new since my last visit was a very attractive garden area developed in the rear. The inn also has its own FM radio station — WFFV-FM 99.3 which the traveller to the Shenandoah Valley can tune in approximately 25 miles from the inn.

The food, prepared by chef Irene Washington, is genuine Southern. Main dishes that I sampled with gusto include the peanut soup and two kinds of ham. The first is a lightly salted baked sugar cured ham served with raisin sauce; the other is the famous Virginia ham served with red-eyed gravy. In addition to the ham, there is a very tender and juicy southern fried chicken, beef burgundy, duck l'orange, shrimp creole and spoon bread which is a speciality.

Irene, and her husband Herman, who are the mainstays of the kitchen, now have their two daughters,

Nancy and Pat, cooking under their supervision at the inn. This is the fifth generation of cooks in the family.

The Wayside Inn is an interesting combination of history, comfortable accommodations, delectable food, and a countryside that has dozens of attractive back roads. It is just a short drive to the northern entrance to the Blue Ridge Parkway.

In the summertime, Middletown also enjoys the Wayside Summer Theatre with a professional company of actors.

Middletown is also the location of an outstanding restoration of the National Trust, Belle Grove, which was built in 1794 with architectural refinements suggested by Thomas Jefferson. During the Battle of Cedar Creek the house served as the northern headquarters of General Philip Sheridan.

WAYSIDE INN, since 1797, Middletown, Va. 22645; 703-869-1797. A country resort-inn in the Shenandoah Valley on Rte. 11, just off I-81 (Exit 77). About 1½ hrs. from Washington, D.C. Lodgings. Breakfast, lunch, dinner served daily to travelers. Professional Summer Stock Theatre June 5 — Sept. 20. Herbert White, Innkeeper.

GRAVES MOUNTAIN LODGE, Syria

"Many people that come back again request the rooms that we have with fireplaces," explained Rachel Graves. "It seems to go with our little valley." Jim Graves passed the plate of pancakes fresh from the kitchen. I spooned out some of the golden scrambled eggs and selected some long, inviting strips of bacon from the platter.

"This is the time of year when the fireplace feels mighty good at the end of the day," he said. "I think the foliage is just about at its height." He pointed down into the valley where the creek was flowing serenely. "It looks gentle now," he said, "but we had two serious floods this year. In fact, for awhile we were marooned on this side of the stream."

"I wish you could have been here during our Apple Festival," remarked Rachel, pouring another cup of marvelous coffee. "People came and picked their own apples, and we had a big pot of Brunswick stew going, and they came from all over, just for the fun of being out on the

farm. And you know, some of the kids had never seen
apple trees before. Then they went over to the farm to
look at the pigs and the cattle. For many of them it was
the first farm experience."

Graves Mountain Lodge nestles at the end of the
road in Syria, Virginia, right up against the Blue Ridge
Mountains. At one time the road ran to the other side
of the mountains, but when the Blue Ridge Parkway was
built, the road was closed. Now this valley is a sort of
cloistered place that has a three-thousand-acre working
farm and a country inn.

The accommodations are clean but quite rustic, even
to the point of having to walk outdoors a few steps to
the Wash House for a shower. There are "facilities", however, with each room.

Jim explained that a new lodge was being built that
would probably be ready during the summer of 1973,
and at the same time there was a good possibility of the
GML season being extended.

"We find a great many people would like to come
here during what we call our 'off season,' because it is
so quite and peaceful, and it is possible to get close to
nature."

Actually, Graves Mountain Lodge is a most reasonable two-hour drive from Washington, D.C., but as far
removed as possible from things urban. On this gorgeous
November day the colors were at their best, and at the
same time the grass and willow trees were still green. I
would spend the day wandering around the farm and
hiking back up into the foothills of the Blue Ridge,

taking much care to be certain that I would be back in time for the magnificent family-style meals that are served by the fresh-faced young people, who still apparently believe in the hard work ethic.

GRAVES MOUNTAIN LODGE, Syria, Va. 22743; 703-923-4231. A secluded resort inn on Rte. 231 and 670, 10 mi. north of Madison, Va.; 38 mi. N.W. from Charlottesville, Va. American Plan. Rustic lodgings. Breakfast, lunch, dinner — served to travelers with reservations. Closed Dec. — Mar. James Graves, Innkeeper.

LAKEVIEW LODGE, Roanoke

Anita Lee was telling me about the Old South weekends that are held during January, February and March at the Lakeview Lodge.

"Well, everybody arrives on Friday afternoon and after a little get-together we have dinner at the Club on Friday night. There is dixieland music and dancing and you would be surprised at how quickly everyone gets acquainted. We're on a first name basis in almost no time at all.

"On Saturday morning everyone meets at the Feed Box for breakfast and the day's activities are planned

around the guests' interest. They can play golf, as you know we have 18 holes right here, there's tennis nearby and there are all kinds of back roads leading up into the Blue Ridge. Each of the little towns around here seem to have a lot of antique shops. One of the favorite trips is to Natural Bridge.

"Saturday nights are great fun with a country buffet and dancing.

"On Sunday morning we have a big, big breakfast in the Feed Box and afterward it is just like farewells on shipboard. Everyone is remembering the good time

Natural Bridge, Va.

they've had and there's lots of new friendships made. Of course, a great many people come back each year. I think a lot of people enjoy the activity, but you'd be surprised how many people just come to enjoy the pretty change of scenery and our very early Spring. They don't have to do anything, if they don't want to."

I was very much impressed by some of the imaginative remodeling that was being done in the Lakeview Club. Among other things, a patio has been created for outdoor dining overlooking the golf fairways. Anita explained that the entire property is a former horse show farm. A lot of the farm buildings have been converted to its present use as a resort inn.

"Well this Club was actually one of our main barns," she said. "As you see, some of the stalls have been retained, but I doubt very much if you've ever seen a horse barn with such elegant wallpaper? The fabric was imported from France, laminated in New York and brought to the Lakeview in panels."

We stood for a moment half-way up a most unusual flying staircase that leads up to the second floor. Through the spacious, almost-cathedral window, we had a view of some of the extensive Lakeview grounds, and off in the distance the famous peaks of Otter.

There are two restaurants at Lakeview. One is the Feed Box, where homey, family-style meals are served. The decorations are all very "horsey" and even the menu is printed on a brown bag. They make appropriate souvenirs. The other is the Club, where the cuisine is as glamorous as the surroundings.

A trip to Lakeview Lodge isn't complete without watching the geese and ducks which are in the pond directly in front of the main entrance. Anita also pointed out a growing group of bantam roosters with their shiny, gay feathers.

"They have the run of the place," she said. That's why I heard a rooster crow the next morning.

At Lakeview Lodge I can extend Fall quite a few weeks later, and meet Spring a few weeks earlier.

LAKEVIEW LODGE, Roanoke, Va. 24019; 703-366-0321. A resort inn including golf course, on Rtes. 11 & 220; Exit 43 on I-81. 1 mi. north of Roanoke. Lodgings. Breakfast, lunch, dinner served daily.

West Virginia

*I*n *this issue the number of country inns in West Virginia advances from three to five with the addition of one in Berkeley Springs, which is in the very northeast corner entirely surrounded by Maryland. The other is in the fashionable resort mountains near White Sulphur Springs at Lewisburg. The best road from Virginia to Lewisburg is Route 60 through Clifton Forge and Covington.*

PARK VIEW INN, Berkeley Springs

My son, Keith, was driving as we pulled out of the parking lot at the Park View and drove past the little park (from whence it derives its name) and the bath house immediately next door.

"You know," he said, "I had a good time there. I think that Mr. and Mrs. Barker know how to talk to people and make them feel welcome."

I'm sure that the reason why Jack and Adele Barker communicated so readily not only with my twenty-year-old son, but also with all other guests was because they have spent the major part of their lives in school work.

They both are very warm-hearted, with beautiful manners. I like Adele's gentleness and laughing eyes.

Acquisition of the Park View Inn was for the Barkers the culmination of a long-hoped-for dream. They had been guests there some years ago, and had always hoped that someday perhaps they might own a country inn like the Park View.

Well, it all came true, and believe me they have put their hearts, hands, minds, and inspiration to work. The best parallel I can make would be to say that it is quite reminiscent of Frank Conklin's New London Inn in New Hampshire insofar as cleanliness and congeniality are concerned. There are rocking chairs on the pillared front and side porches, many books in the living room, and a display of photographs of the Berkeley Springs of yesteryear when it was a celebrated, fashionable health resort.

Today, as in those days, besides the very beautiful mountains, deep valleys and winding streams, the attraction for Berkeley Springs are the Baths. These are maintained by the state, and it is still possible to have a vapor bath, a hot tub and massage, at a most reasonable cost. Many of the Park View guests find this refreshing at any time of the day.

As we drove into the countryside, Keith said, "I hope you're going to tell about the food." Indeed I am. It is the best of West Virginia cooking, including baked chicken, country ham, biscuits, and three kinds of vegetables, each of them cooked with something special. For example, in the carrots I recognized the light touch of both ginger and lemon.

Some of the photographs indicated that there is a very considerable snowfall in this section of the country which gave rise to the idea that it would be a good place to come and do some cross-country skiing. It is just about two hours from Washington.

PARK VIEW INN, Berkeley Springs, W. Va. 25411; 304-258-2210. A mountain resort inn on Rte. 522, 34 mi. from Winchester, Va. and 96 mi. from Washington, D.C. Berkeley Springs Spa adjoins inn. Lodgings. American and European Plan. Breakfast, lunch, dinner served to travelers. xc skiing. Open every day in the year. Jack and Adele Barker, Innkeepers.

FARAWAY HILLS, Beverly

I believe that I have received as many complimentary letters about Faraway Hills as any other inn in "Country Inns and Back Roads." This is interesting, because it is deep in the West Virginia mountains, and not accessible by super-highways.

"Mac" and Eleanor McManus started this inn a number of years ago and set a standard that country inns everywhere would do well to emulate. Now the new owners, Fred and Carol Allen, who are originally from Pennsylvania and are two very attractive young people, are continuing to operate Faraway Hills in the McManus tradition. They both have a very healthy interest in antiques and have added their collection to those already in use in the inn. I found that they had a capacity for hard work which is very refreshing.

During 1972, their first full year of operation, with Mrs. McManus also on deck, they needed to be very hard workers! Apparently three years of teaching school for each of them in Butler, Pennsylvania was good training.

Faraway Hills has four things to recommend it most highly. For one thing, there is the outstanding scenery which is visible from all windows and porches of the inn. Second, there is a real farmland feeling which Jan has captured in this sketch of the barn and wagon which are to be found in the rear of the inn. Third, the warm hospitality which is always evident to me as soon as I step inside. Fourth, there is the food about which I have written many times in the past. Sufficeth it to say at this time that it still continues to draw people through those mountains in all kinds of weather, and in three out of four seasons to return again and again.

Perhaps the final quality is found in the guests themselves, who, because they have found in Faraway Hills a kind of country inn that has so much appeal for them, all share in a common experience.

The decor, which has a great deal to do with the way we feel about an inn, is not rustic like Graves Mountain Lodge in Syria, Virginia, nor is it elegant like the Jared Coffin House in Nantucket, Massachusetts. It is a rather simple Victorian style with a great deal of emphasis on extra little touches such as flowers on the table and gleaming napery. The kitchen, by the way, is open for everyone to enjoy.

Inaccessible? Not really for the adventuresome traveler. Is it worth it? Well, I have a file full of letters from people who vehemently insist that it is.

FARAWAY HILLS, Box 698, Beverly, West Va. 26253; 304-636-0800. A country inn 6 mi. south of Elkins, West Va., Rtes. 219, 250. Adjacent to the scene of the first battle of the Civil War at Rich Mountain. Lodgings. Breakfast served only to house guests. Dinner served every day from March 16 to Dec. 14th. Fred Allen, Innkeeper.

GENERAL LEWIS INN, Lewisburg

I had just returned from a walking tour of Lewisburg with its old 19th century residences and generous sprinkling of historic markers. I paused for just a moment at the bottom of the crescent-shaped walk that leads to the inn, to read a marker which said, "Confederate troops under General Henry Heth on May 23, 1862 were repulsed by Colonel George Crook's Brigade."

As I settled into one of the rocking chairs on the long, shaded veranda, Innkeeper Larry Little came out and joined me.

"Well, what do you think of our little town?" he said. I readily admitted that I was completely captivated.

"It was established in 1782, and is the third oldest town in the state," he said. "It was named for General Andrew Lewis, who defeated the Indians at the first battle in the American Revolution in 1774.

"The old part of the inn where the dining room is located was built in 1798 as a private dwelling. Later on, additions were made, and in 1929 it was opened by Mr. and Mrs. Randolph Hock as an inn. It took them many years to collect all of these antiques, including that four-poster, canopy bed you are going to sleep in tonight."

The General Lewis Inn, which is moderate in both size and tariff, is like a permanent flashback to the many historical epochs associated with West Virginia. The presence of many Confederate flags attest to a keen interest in that aspect. It is almost entirely furnished in antiques, and there is a sizeable collection of old kitchen utensils, spinning wheels, prints, churns, and other tools used many years ago. There is an unusual collection of chinaware. The parlor has a very friendly fireplace flanked by some of the many different types of rocking chairs that are scattered throughout the inn. Things are made even more cozy by the low beamed ceilings which came from log cabins on the inn grounds.

The inn is surrounded by broad lawns, and in the rear there are aromatic Southern gardens and tall swaying trees, in the midst of which is a small rock garden.

The menu has many things that I associate with the South — pork chops and applesauce, pan-fried chicken, and West Virginia country ham, to name a few.

Dusk had fallen while Larry, Mrs. Hock and I were talking, and the gaslights which illuminate the tree-lined streets began to dot the late twilight. Our talk turned to some of the famous golf courses here in the Greenbrier area, and we discussed some circle tours of these southern mountains that would include the fabulous scenery and also a generous glimpse of rural West Virginia.

"More and more people are discovering what we've got down here," he said, "or up here, as the case may be."

GENERAL LEWIS INN, Lewisburg, West Va. 24901; 304-645-2600. An antique-laden village inn on Rte. 60, 90 mi. from Roanoke. Lodgings. Breakfast and dinner served daily, with three meals on Sundays. Open daily except Christmas. Lawrence Little, Innkeeper.

WELLS INN, Sistersville

"I think it must be something of a record for a town of our size," stated Jack Kinkaid. "If they're all accepted I'm sure it will be a wonderful thing."

Jack and I were standing in front of the red brick Wells Inn of which he is the innkeeper. We were speaking of the fact that both the Wells Inn and the Sistersville Municipal Building were given a listing in the National Register of Historic Places by the United States Department of Interior. He was referring to the fact that Sistersville has six other sites which have been nominated for listing.

"I think we are relatively untouched both by progress and by change," he went on. "Before 1899 Sistersville provided services for the surrounding farm community and was a stop-over point for the steamboat trade on the Ohio. However, oil was discovered by two brothers, and our population went up from 500 to over 13,000 people, and there were derricks everywhere. We returned to being a small community in 1915 when the oil boom ended, and I guess our population is about 2,300 today."

The Wells Inn fits perfectly into the pattern created by the Victorian and Greek revival architecture of the town itself. It was built in 1894 and essentially reflects a straight late Victorian utilitarianism in the rather severe facade which is relieved by a classical porch. When I first stepped into the red carpeted lobby with the heavy mahogany woodwork and the plaster statue of a partially clothed lady named Victoria it was like suddenly being on an old movie set. This decor is maintained throughout in the restored main dining room, the parlors, and also the lodging rooms. I hasten to add, however, that although the appearance of the plumbing is late '90's, the function is early 1970's!

In recent years, Jack has taken a great interest in the food served in the inn dining room. "We've never been afraid to experiment," he asserts. "As a result there are always new items appearing on our menu. We're very fortunate to be able to draw from the rich farming country in Ohio for fresh fruits and vegetables. We're also well-known for our homemade pastries and pies."

To top off the entire Sistersville experience, it is still possible to arrive and depart from the beautiful Ohio countryside across the river on the Sistersville ferry boat. It reminds me of the ferry at Oxford, Maryland by which I travel to reach the Robert Morris Inn. To add to the flavor, there are usually a couple of old stern wheel river boats anchored on the Ohio side.

WELLS INN, 316 Charles St., Sistersville, West Va. 26175; 304-652-3111. A restored Victorian village inn 50 mi. south of Wheeling, 38 mi. north of Parkersburg. Sistersville is a former oil boom town of the '90's. Lodgings. Breakfast, lunch, dinner served daily. Jack Kinkaid, Innkeeper.

DROVERS INN, Wellsburg

Mary Marko and I had driven over to Meadowcroft Village for a few moments because she wanted to show me some of the newly-completed restored buildings. We stopped at the one-room schoolhouse which was built in 1834, and I took the opportunity to pull the rope and toll the old school bell.

Meadowcroft in Avella, Pennsylvania is just a few miles from the Drover's Inn in Wellsburg, West Virginia where Mary is the innkeeper.

The history of the inn goes back to 1848 when it was built by John Fowler. At that time it was certainly one of the most auspicious structures in that part of the country. For many years it housed Fowler's General Store and the town post office. Fowler's General Store has been reproduced at Meadowcroft Village.

School at Meadowcroft Village

Over a century ago the road in front of the inn was the principal route for drovers moving their stock across the toll road from Pennsylvania and Ohio. At the Drovers Inn they could obtain not only lodging and food for themselves, but also fodder for their livestock which were kept in pens adjacent to the inn.

Today, the inn reflects Mary's work and devotion in restoring it. On the main floor are two contrasting dining rooms, one informal with interesting bric-a-brac, advertisements, old calendars, pictures and posters. It has red-checked tablecloths. The other dining room is a more formal Victorian room, with handsome tables, each with its own individual set of matched chairs.

The mellowed red brick building is set back from the road amongst trees and with a beautiful view from the lawn in the rear.

Mary takes great pride in showing her guests through the inn, and she has left one room exactly the way she found it seven years ago when she took over the inn.

I found the best way to get to Wellsburg from Washington, Pennsylvania is on Rte. 844 which passes through Wolfdale, Buffalo and Middletown. At the Pennsylvania border it becomes West Va. Rte. 27. It has no lodging rooms and serves dinners only from Wednesday through Sunday. It is quite an experience.

DROVERS INN, Washington Pike, Wellsburg, West Va. 26070; 304-737-0188. A country restaurant in a historic building on Rte. W. Va. 27, 16 mi. north of Wheeling and 18 mi. from Washington, Pa. Near Meadowcroft Village, Avella, Pa. No lodgings. Dinner only served daily from Wednesday through Sunday. Closed Christmas. Mary Marko, Innkeeper.

Kentucky

In addition to the Shaker Restoration at Pleasant Hill, and the college inn at Berea, we discovered three inns that were new to us in the Blue Grass State. We spent a memorable night at a forest-surrounded inn in Doe Run, had a lip smacking repast at a restaurant on the shores of the Ohio at Louisville, and dipped back into the heritage of the South in Shelbyville.

INN AT PLEASANT HILL, Shakertown

Betty Morris and I had walked down the country street to visit some new buildings and were now approaching the Trustee's House. She pointed to the small, dormer window which protruded from the third floor. "There's an interesting little sideline about that window," she said. "As you know, the Shakers were strong believers in celibacy, and in order to make certain that the rule was adhered to, some of the buildings had special windows for 'watching'."

The Shakers founded the Pleasant Hill experiment early in the 19th century, and it flourished here for almost a century. Fortunately, the years did not take a heavy toll, although certain property was sold off from time to time in a number of comparatively small tracts.

Betty explained that leading citizens of the area had long hoped to restore the village and in 1961 Shakertown at Pleasant Hill, Kentucky Inc., an organization dedicated to that end, was formed.

"This group purchased the land containing 23 buildings and over 2000 acres of farmland," she explained. "Cabinetmakers were put to work reproducing Shaker furniture and workmen began installing heat and electric facilities, water, gas and telephone lines. Of course, every effort was made to hide these modern installations in order to preserve the antique character of the village.

"The entire area abounds in trees and shrubs and wildflowers — lobelia, liverwood, and others with which the Shaker sisters made medicine and dyes—grow profusely."

Today, as an integral part of this restored Shaker Village, there is an inn maintained that abounds in the hallmarks of Shaker hospitality.

For example, specialties from the Shaker kitchen include country ham, fried chicken and vegetables grown in the village garden, as well as homemade relishes and such dessert "goodies" as Shaker lemon pie.

The lodging rooms are beautifully simple. They are furnished with reproductions of Shaker beds, chairs and tables. Many of them have Shaker trundle beds as well. Shaker pegs are placed all around each room for hanging clothes. The bedspreads and curtains are also of Shaker design.

I find that Shakertown can be enjoyed in many ways — as a destination for those who just want to look and learn; as a place to dine; as a meeting place for clubs and conventions; as a spot for a pleasant walk and as a place to spend a weekend, a week, or even longer. As far as I know, it is the only restored historic village in the country in which visitors may spend the night in the original buildings.

One of the events that I am looking forward to with great pleasure is the annual meeting of Berkshire Traveller innkeepers and their wives. This year it is going to be held at the Inn at Pleasant Hill at Shakertown, with visits to Science Hill Inn and Boone Tavern Hotel in Berea. We are all anticipating a wonderful time.

INN AT PLEASANT HILL, Shakertown, Ky., P.O. address: Harrodsburg, Ky. 40330; 606-734-9111. A country inn in a restored Shaker village on Rte. 68, 7 mi. northeast of Harrodsburg, 24 mi. southwest of Lexington. Lodgings. Breakfast, lunch, dinner served daily to travelers. Lodgings available every day in the year. Meals served every day except Christmas Eve and Christmas Day. Mrs. Betty Morris, Innkeeper.

SCIENCE HILL INN, Shelbyville

There are two immediately fascinating features about this inn in Shelbyville, Kentucky. The first is the name: Science Hill. The second is the tremendous, arcaded court where I wandered about, while waiting for a table.

Innkeeper Buddy Jones explained that when Julia Tevis came to Kentucky from Virginia in 1824 she acquired the buildings and vowed to teach the young ladies of the surrounding vicinity art and science. Up until then, apparently, the younger female generation was taught little more than the social graces.

"She stood on the bottom of the hill, to the rear of the property," he said, "and declared the name of the school to be 'Science Hill'."

He went on to explain that the earliest history has long been lost to posterity, but, apparently it is possible to date some of the buildings as far back as 1790.

The history of the school is most interesting, as it became one of the outstanding preparatory schools in the country. It flourished until 1939, and during the 114 years girls came from all over the nation to learn and enjoy the quiet dignity and partake of its culture.

The arcaded courtyard, which was once open to the sky, is most unique. Its three stories are ample enough to accommodate a full-grown tree, and the second floor gallery which traverses the sides is reminiscent of earlier times. In the middle, directly under the glass cupola, there is a fountain with a real sense of humor. Cupid is holding a fish which is squirting water in his face! The day I was there the first thing I encountered was a knight in full armor sitting on a horse in full armor. This is part of the unusual group of antiques on display at the Wakefield-Scearce Gallery, which is also under the same roof.

There are no lodgings at Science Hill. Perhaps this would be guilding the lily. The food is on a par with the atmosphere. Menu offerings are a combination of "down country Kentucky" including country ham, baked pork chops, smothered chicken, as well as some more sophisticated offerings.

I think that Miss Julia Tevis would be fascinated to visit Science Hill today. I was.

SCIENCE HILL INN, 525 Washington St., Shelbyville, Ky. 40065; 502-633-2825. An elegant restaurant combined with an equally impressive antiques gallery, 28 mi. east of Louisville. No lodgings. Lunch and dinner served daily except Monday. Closed Christmas through New Years Day. Buddy Jones, Innkeeper.

THE NORMANDY INN, Louisville

I was standing with Paul O'Brien, restauranteur, story-teller, sometimes truck driver, and always the picture of congeniality, on the bank of the Ohio at Louisville just a few paces from 7th and Washington Streets.

"Yes," he said, "there used to be many side wheelers or stern wheelers on the river here, but now I guess they are all gone. The Delta Queen still takes cruises, and every once in a while somebody brings a smaller one out of mothballs. But the halcyon days are gone."

The nostalgia in his voice gave me a clue as to how enthusiastic Paul has been in restoring a building and creating an atmosphere at the Normandy Inn in Louisville. Incidentally, in this issue, there are four inns (in this case a restaurant) that are located in cities which we felt had the real atmosphere and personal involvement that we look for in an inn in the country. The other two are the Algonquin in New York, Lamothe House in New Orleans, and the Brazilian Court in Palm Beach.

Mississippi side wheeler

The Normandy Inn is one part Paul O'Brien, one part restored 19th century building, and one part carefully prepared and unusually interesting food. The building was described in the last issue of "Country Inns and Back Roads," so it now behooves us to take a good look at the menu.

Let's begin with one of the specialties of the house — a black bean soup which has been intelligently augmented with just the right amount of sherry. There is also a soup of the day which is usually most inventive. Among the dishes from France are tender chicken breasts topped with an interesting sauce of cream, blue cheese, minced onions and sliced mushrooms. There is also some very tasty brook trout which has been carefully boned, stuffed with crab and shrimp tidbits, and sprinkled with toasted almonds.

From Denmark there is a roasted loin of suckling pig stuffed with prunes and apples and is adorned with a fine sauce which contains sour cream and currants.

On this particular visit I enjoyed the curried veal a la Normandy, which was diced veal simmered with sliced apples and onions and served over fluffy white rice.

Then there are ribs of beef, lamb chops, steak and beef filets, and some really hard-to-resist-even-if-you-haven't-got-room desserts. Lest I forget, the Hearthstone Tavern next door serves fondue, welsh rarebit, cheese and hamburgers for those who would enjoy a late snack.

It happens that I am writing this particular inn adventure on a cold winter's night in Stockbridge, Mass'tts., a half continent away from Louisville. I'm sure you'll understand if I say I'm getting hungry!—

NORMANDY INN, 7th and Washington Sts., Louisville, Ky. 40202; 502-585-2849. A country restaurant on the Louisville waterfront. Lunch: Mon-Fri.; Dinner: Mon-Sat. (Closed for lunch on Sat. and all day Sun.) Paul O'Brien, Innkeeper.

DOE RUN INN, Brandenburg

I turned off the light and settled down into the incredibly huge mahogany bed. My eyes got used to the darkness, and I could see the outlines of the antique chairs and the rug. The light from the little chunk stove cast reflections on the thick stone outer walls. As I remained still for a few moments I could hear two owls hooting in the forest outside.

It was interesting to realize that Abraham Lincoln's father actually helped build the original part of the old mill which is now the Doe Run Inn. I couldn't help but think of the rustic similarity to Graves Mountain Lodge in Syria, Virginia. For example, neither have telephones in the rooms, or T.V. (There is an ancient telephone booth downstairs for private calls.)

Naturally, a building of this size that has been converted to lodging rooms and bathrooms has had to undergo some changes — the installation of water pipes, electric lines and some heating facilities — but happily these are kept at a minimum while the guests still enjoy their convenience.

If the lodgings are unique, certainly the food is equally so. When I arrived earlier, just about dinnertime, the aroma from the kitchen, especially of the fried chicken, was almost too much. I also detected the Kentucky fried ham which is served with red-eye gravy and hot biscuits. On Friday and Sunday this highly atmospheric inn serves an "all you can eat" smorgasbord.

Although the light was failing fast, after dinner I took a short walk in the woods, which cover over one thousand acres and assure continuous privacy and quietude. Afterwards, I joined the other guests in the big downstairs living room with the bright fireplace. Some had been returning for many years in succession.

To illustrate my point I would like to quote from a letter I received from one of our readers in East Aurora, New York:

"That night we arrived at the Doe Run Inn in time for a late dinner. I have never tasted such chicken and ham, and the biscuits almost floated off the plate. We had lemon pie for dessert which simply defies description. Everyone was very friendly, including the dog. We had the most delightful room with two double beds in it, and our own private bath. Three of us had a hilarious time over the fact that the water faucets were reversed. Nobody told anybody else, and we all discovered it the hard way when we took showers; I wondered if the inn had a ghost, but decided not to ask! The next morning we had a wonderful breakfast including beaten biscuits and grits."

DOE RUN INN, Brandenburg, Ky. 40108; 502-422-2042. A country inn reminiscent of the backwoods on Rte. 448, 4 mi. south of Brandenburg, 38 mi. south of Louisville. Near Fort Knox. Lodgings. Breakfast, lunch and dinner. Closed Christmas Eve and Christmas Day. Curtis and Lucille Brown, Innkeepers.

BOONE TAVERN HOTEL, Berea

This letter was from Michigan, and it was typical of letters that I receive from many other states concerning visits to Berea.

"I had never heard of Berea College or Berea, Kentucky or the Boone Tavern Hotel. But after reading about all of them in your book, my husband and I changed our routes on the way south to go through central Kentucky for a look.

"We were enchanted with all three. You said that you wished you could send your son to Berea, well we talked seriously about moving to that area so that our daughter could apply. What a group of attractive, self-reliant students!

"And that hotel, why it is as neat as a pin, and those student waitresses are so sweet and appealing. They even refuse tips! The furniture in our bedroom was all made by students in their workshop — copies of authentic early colonial furniture. We just could not get over it.

"We purchased one of Mr. Hougen's three cookbooks, and as soon as I could get to a stove I tried several recipes. Particularly that spoon bread! Those lady cooks of his in the hotel put me to shame.

"Speaking of food, we also adored that southern peanut soup, baked plantation ham and escalloped okra.

"We toured the campus and saw all the student industries: broom craft, fireside weaving, ceramics, furniture making — well everything. We were impressed beyond words."

"Mr. Hougen explained that Berea College serves the youth of 230 mountain counties in the 8 southern states, the region known as Appalachia. Eighty per cent of the students are from the region and are chosen on the basis of financial need, high scholastic standing and character. The other twenty per cent come from the states and many from Europe, Asia, and Africa. He also explained that the inn is owned by the

Berea College chapel

college and one of the opportunities that the students have to work ten hours a week is in the hotel in one of the many different jobs. Many of his students major in hotel management and have been very successful in the hotel business.

"I was also glad that we were there during the time that "Wilderness Road" by Paul Green, which is a drama depicting the founding of Berea College, was being shown. It is presented June 26 through September 3rd.

"This was our first visit to a Berkshire Traveller Inn. Believe me, we are going to try all of them."

Thank you very much.

BOONE TAVERN HOTEL, Berea, Kentucky 40403; 606-986-3154. A village inn in a unique college community on I-75, 40 mi. south of Lexington, Kentucky. Lodgings. Breakfast, lunch, dinner served every day to travelers. (By sittings only). Never closed. Richard Hougen, Innkeeper.

Dress Regulation: Coats for men, dresses or well tailored pant suits for ladies, Sunday noons and evening dinners.

North Carolina

We have a bonanza of four new country inns in western North Carolina in this edition. The first is in Burnsville, which is north of Asheville on Rte. 19. Two of the other three are west of Asheville off Rte. 19 at Bryson City and Robbinsville. The fourth is reached by turning south off Route 19 to Route 28 through Franklin and some unbelievably beautiful country to Highlands. It is possible to take the Blue Ridge Parkway to this section of western Carolina, but the speed limit is only 45 miles per hour and it is a narrow two lane highway. However, it is well worth the slow trip.

COLONIAL INN, Hillsborough

I am a menu saver, and I have a drawer with nothing but menus from my favorite country inns. By reading

them over, I can go back in my mind's eye to my last visit.

I was shuffling through these menus during the winter and ran across one from the Colonial Inn in Hillsborough, North Carolina. At the Colonial Inn, the big emphasis is on home cooked, southern country food. Their menu includes:

Country-cured ham with applesauce, roast round of beef with brown gravy, old-fashioned chicken with dumplings, roast leg of lamb with mint jelly, salmon croquettes, and flounder stuffed with King crabmeat. Included with the entree is a choice of two of the many fresh vegetables which appear on the menu; and for dessert there is blackberry, apple, or peach cobbler, Colonial frozen vanilla Delight, or a lemon tart served with whipped cream.

The Colonial Inn is an unassuming village inn whose history dates back to the occupation by the British under Lord Cornwallis. Although the lodgings are neat, they don't pretend to "put on airs." In the last edition Jan sketched the outside of the inn showing its second floor balcony. This time she has sketched the living room with the fireplace and antique country furniture.

The Colonial Inn is in the attractive little town of Hillsborough in eastern North Carolina. This town was one of the most prominent of the Revolutionary War period since it was the capital of North Carolina at one time. The inn is in the center of town and the many historic homes, churches and public buildings are within a leisurely walking distance. The gardens of Hillsborough, many of which were planned during the days of the great estates, feature boxwoods,, roses and flowering shrubs. Innkeeper Pete Thompson explained to me that old bulbs come up everywhere in the Hillsborough gardens, bearing witness to the love of the early settlers for their homes in England.

The Colonial Inn and Hillsborough, North Carolina are another fine example of an inn and a community being well matched.

COLONIAL INN, 153 W. King St., Hillsborough, N.C. 27278; 919-732-2461. A village inn with modest lodgings in a town with much history. 11 mi. from Durham and Chapel Hill. Lodgings. Lunch and dinner served every day except Christmas, Easter Monday, 4th of July and Labor Day. V.V. "Pete" Thompson, Innkeeper.

For *anyone who has never been to western North Carolina, Asheville, and the Great Smokies, I can say without any equivocation that it will be a truly memorable experience. The best word to describe it is "spectacular." The mountains are the highest in eastern America, and as I understand it, the oldest in the world. There are more varieties of flowers and trees than anywhere outside of China. Just outside of Highlands, N.C. are the sheerest cliffs in eastern America, 1800 feet high. There are gems to be found throughout the area, and I was amazed at how people participate in gem and rock hunting. There are marvelously fantastic roads, twisting up, down, over, and between these mountains which live up to the name given them by the Indians because of the almost constant cloud formations above them. The area has the largest birch, spruce, and hardwood forests in the United States. It is the scene of the original home of the Cherokee Indians before they were unmercifully routed up and taken further west. In fact, the Cherokee Reservation still covers a tremendous number of acres. The season is long, and the weather is well balanced in the summer time. Fortunately, I found several excellent country inns, each of them with its own personality.*

HOUND EARS LODGE, Blowing Rock

There are a few places mentioned in this book which may seem as far removed from the concept of a New England country inn as Stockbridge is from Sydney, Australia. These include the Algonquin Hotel in New York, the Wigwam in Phoenix, and Hound Ears Lodge in Blowing Rock, North Carolina. I was persuaded that, although these places were not all that quaint or particularly ancient, they did have some of the qualities for which I search in a country inn. These included warmth, involvement, and the opportunity to meet and enjoy myself with other people.

It is my assumption that there are several different kinds of country inns and resort inns. I enjoy myself at all of the inns featured in this book, and from the volume of my correspondence about the three inns mentioned above, apparently there are a number of people who share my enthusiasm.

Hound Ears is a full American Plan resort inn. The emphasis is on some great golf, marvelous scenery, and in the winter, some excellent skiing both on the grounds and nearby. It is an inn for adults with an active interest in outdoor activity such as golf, tennis, swimming and walking in the peaceful woods. Because there are so many activities nearby such as the Tweetsie Railroad and the Land of Oz, the younger generation finds it to their liking as well. I met and talked to quite a few families on my visits.

Hound Ears is tucked away in a valley of the high country of North Carolina's Blue Ridge Mountains. Many people who visit there eventually buy houses which dot the surrounding mountainside.

All of the furnishings and appointments, both interior and exterior, are carefully thought out and harmonized. For example, my tree-top chalet was done in compatible shades of brown. I had yellow sheets on my bed. All of the buildings were set among magnolia and evergreen trees, and in many places huge boulders were allowed to remain where they rested, and the road was built around them, curving, twisting and ever-climbing.

It is difficult in mid-summer when experiencing the verdant greens and fairways punctuated by the clear white, menacing sand traps, to realize that everything is covered by many inches of snow almost every Christmas and that the other face of Hound Ears, the winter visage, is one that includes spectacular alpine and cross-country skiing, roaring fireplaces and the exhilaration of pure winter air.

HOUND EARS LODGE AND CLUB, P.O. Box 277, Blowing Rock, N.C. 28605; 704-963-4321. A luxurious resort inn on Rte. 105, 6 mi. from Boone. 18-hole golf course. Near several ski areas and natural attractions. American Plan. Meals to house guests only. Alpine and xc ski. Mildred Bunting, Innkeeper.

NU-WRAY INN, Burnsville

There was a noise. An insistent urging, cajoling clang of a bell. I awakened from my sound sleep in my somewhat austere bedroom on the third floor of the Nu-Wray Inn and realized that Rush Wray, the intrepid innkeeper, was informing all of his house guests that it was 8 A.M., and it was thirty minutes before breakfast.

About 29½ minutes later I stumbled down the stairway into the main living room where I found all the other house guests seated on the various types of Carolina antique furniture that Rush has scattered around informally, all shaking their heads and saying the same thing:

"I don't know how he does it. This is the only place I've ever been to where they wake you up with a bell." In just a few moments the bell rang once again, this time with our genial host standing in the hallway at the entrance to the dining room. Upon that signal we all ventured forth like a group of hungry hippopotami, to be greeted in the main dining room by the most magnificent sight that I could imagine at that hour of the morning — great long tables with white tablecloths covered with platters of scrambled eggs, steaming pancakes, warm syrup, country ham, grits, applesauce, hot biscuits, apple butter, great compotes of honey, and tubs of fresh country butter.

Rush introduced all of the newcomers, and we all sat down to pass the food, laugh and joke, and eat a breakfast that would delight a trencherman.

What a fantastic way to start the day in the North Carolina mountains!

There are two meals a day served at the Nu-Wray; the other is dinner and it is at six-thirty and reservations are necessary: There is just one sitting, and if you are not there when the bell rings, you've missed it.

This is the first edition in which we have talked about the Nu-Wray although I sent many people there after my visit during the summer of 1972. I've heard from many of them, and they all have the same comment: "It's unbelievable!"

The Nu-Wray is where there are old-fashioned door keys, and every guest returns his to the old-fashioned key rack in the lobby. There is a big fireplace at one end, and many, many antiques, including rockers. There is an old Regina, which is an old-fashioned music box that has metal discs. On the second floor there is a very charming drawing room furnished with family antiques. When I was there, there was an art class from Ohio, and we all had a marvelous time after dinner listening to the critique of the instructor.

There are many, many things to be said about Mr. Rush Wray and the Nu-Wray Inn in Burnsville, North Carolina. I'm looking forward very much to unfolding the story in future editions. However, I think it can all be summed up in the words of my fellow New Englander, Mr. Thoreau. I found this quotation in a framed plaque on the wall: "If a man does not keep pace with his companions, it is because he is listening to a different drummer."

At the Nu-Wray Inn everyone steps to the music of a definitely different drummer.

NU-WRAY INN, Box 156, Burnsville, N.C. 28714; 704-682-2329. A village inn on Rte 19E, 38 mi. north of Ashville. A few miles from Mt. Mitchell. Lodgings. American Plan, Mod. American Plan and European Plan. Breakfast and dinner served to travelers. Reservations preferred. Breakfast and dinner at noon on Sunday, no Sunday evening meal. Open every day of the year. Rush T. Wray, Innkeeper, Mrs. Annie Wray Bennett, hostess.

HEMLOCK INN, Bryson City

"It's just like havin' company all the time." Ella Jo Shell was explaining the way that she and John felt about owning the Hemlock Inn high up in the foothills of the Great Smokies. We were seated at the open end of the large room that serves as a combination dining room and sitting room. It overlooks a beautiful view of the mountains.

"John and I are both from Marietta, Georgia and ever since the first time we came up to these mountains all that we ever wanted to do was find a way to live here permanently. The previous owner, knowing that John was in the insurance and investment business, asked for help in finding a buyer."

At this point, John, who is a very soft spoken Georgian, entered and continued her narrative.

"The next day I called him and said, 'I think I found a buyer for your inn . . . . me!" We all laughed, and I felt as though I had known the Shells for much longer than the short time since my arrival. It's the way they are — warm, outgoing, considerate and highly involved with their guests.

This is best illustrated by the fact that breakfast and dinner, which are the two meals served at the Hemlock Inn, are served at large Lazy Susan tables which accommodate twelve or more. Everything is served family style, and every effort is made to see that guests sit at a different table for every meal. This makes getting acquainted a very simple and very happy process.

John summed it up somewhat by saying: "We don't have a swimming pool, television or a golf course. But, what we do have is a plain old mountain inn where folks can just be themselves and unwind. We find that when they come here first they are frequently very tired and grumpy, but after a couple of days of this mountain air and our good cooking, they are as happy as a lark."

The Hemlock Inn, like so many country inns, is a family affair, with John and Ella Jo and their youngest daughter, Lainey, pitching in to do a little of everything. There are three local ladies to do the cooking. Just as the case at the Nu-Wray Inn, guests are summoned to meals by a bell, and since the dinner is served at six, there is plenty of daylight left for shuffleboard or skittles or just sitting and rocking and looking at the mountains.

I discovered that inns in the southern highlands often have very few extensive on-the-scene facilities. In a great many ways they are a return to the true innkeeping of the 18th and 19th centuries when folks set a great store on visiting and talking, maybe singing songs or telling stories, and doing lots of laughing.

It suits me just fine.

HEMLOCK INN, Bryson City, N.C. 28713; 704-488-9820. A mountain inn just off Rte. 19, 60 mi. from Ashville, in the middle of the Great Smokies. Lodgings. Mod. American Plan. Meals to travelers by reservation only Open early May to early November. Ella Jo and John Shell, Innkeepers.

SNOWBIRD MOUNTAIN LODGE, Robbinsville

I really couldn't speak. The entire aspect was so awesome and so majestic that the spoken word seemed crushing to the mood. I was standing on the broad balcony of the Snowbird Mountain Lodge at twilight. Against a backdrop of delicate, iridescent blue, the silhouettes of the mute mountain peaks seemed to thunder at me. I could almost reach out and touch at least fifteen of them. Their heights were awesome — 4000 ft., 4500 ft., 4700 ft., 5400 ft.! The drop-off in front of me was 1000 feet straight down into a lake whose waters were so clear that in full daylight I could see the bottom. A mountain whippoorwill greeted a quarter moon that even now was becoming more bright.

I stepped back inside the beautiful, high-vaulted living room and went over to join the people standing and sitting around the mammoth fireplace. It was easy to fall into the conversation because most of them were talking about the day's hiking and comparing notes about the various flowers and birds. This is seventh heaven for birders. Among the flowers are flame azaleas and mountain laurel.

I found to reach the SML required persistence, patience and trust. I drove from Saluda on Rte. 19, through the Cherokee Reservation and the Nantahala Gorge. There I saw people riding the rapids in rubber rafts right next to the highway. I found Rte. 129 cut back into the mountains to Robbinsville, and from then on I trusted the signs.

I came to the foot of a hill where there was a little sign that pointed to the left that said: "Snowbird Mountain Lodge." This was a paved, single-lane road with many signs that said: "Blow Your Horn." At the top of the mountain is perched this remote resort inn.

Because this is a mountain inn, there is naturally a great deal of emphasis on hiking and back roading. To that end, Mary and Ed can supply all of their guests with maps for both hiking and driving in the area. Incidentally, there is a small Indian reservation nearby. The atmosphere is quite informal and sport clothes are the order of the day. However, I was glad I had some warm clothes, because even in summer the temperatures averaged in the 70's.

It didn't take Ed and Mary very long to discover that every one of the guests returned at the end of the day with ravenous appetites. In a letter I received late in the season from them they said that their Saturday night buffets were very popular and that the Sunday morning buffet breakfasts were a huge success. They also provide box lunches for guests who are going to be gone during the day in the woods.

It should be pointed out that although this is wild and quite primitive land, there is no need for anyone to feel chary about venturing into the woods as long as they stick to the trails and act sensibly. It can really be a great experience.

One final note: Ed Williams says: "At SML don't step back to get a better look!"

SNOWBIRD MOUNTAIN LODGE, Joyce Kilmer Forest Rd., Robbinsville, N.C. 28771; 704-479-3433. An inn on the top of the mountain in the Great Smokies. 12 mi. from Robbinsville. Lodgings. American Plan. Lunch and dinner served to travelers by reservation only. Open May 1st through October 31st. Mary and Ed Williams, Innkeepers.

LEE'S INN, Highlands

Lee's Inn in Highlands, North Carolina is a delightful soupçon of elegance. In the short time that I was a guest, I had a generous glimpse of those qualities of which the South is most justifiably proud: good manners, good taste and good humor.

The town of Highlands is really most unusual. It is the highest elevated town east of Denver, and to reach it from any of the four directions it is necessary to point the car uphill. Coming down from the north, I passed striking cascades, impressive chasms and awesome rock formations. It is quite a surprise to find such a genteel, well-planned community at the top of the mountains.

Lee's Inn is within the town, but off the main thoroughfare. A spacious white building with an outer second floor gallery, it sets amongst the trees with a welcome swimming pool just off the front porch.

It so happened that I was the only Yankee in the house, however, the hostess, who for all the world seemed like one of the guests, made sure that we all got acquainted. I was immediately included in some amusing parlor games and then invited to join some very lovely people from Atlanta for dinner. It was all very natural and relaxed.

Here the real picture of the inn unfolded. There seemed to be dozens of families with small children. It was really a very impressive scene. Everybody was well dressed, and the soft southern accents were interspersed with frequent bursts of laughter. There seemed to be a very happy rapport between the guests, particularly the children, and the dining room staff.

It was explained to me that many of these people have been coming to the inn for a number of years because it provides a real vacation for every member of the family. The inn maintains a very good youth activities program which provides energetic and sympathetic counsellors to keep these children entertained with all kinds of activities during the day. This allows mother and dad to play golf at the famous nearby courses or sit around the pool or pursue their own preferences. There are also tennis courts nearby.

Everybody meets for dinner and family activity at the end of the day. It works out marvelously.

One of the things that interests almost every visitor to Highlands, regardless fo age, is gem hunting. I'll admit that it seemed rather strange to me at first — the idea of getting a bucket of mud and then getting myself all dirty running water through it and looking for bits of sapphires, emeralds, and other semi-precious stones. Well, believe me, everybody does it, and the talk at the dinner tables about the various kinds of stones that were found was not confined to the children!

Since my first visit to Lee's Inn, and before this edition of CIBR was published, I told many people about it personally. Some of them went many miles out of their way to have the experience, and I am delighted to say that the opinion is unanimous.

LEE'S INN, Highlands, N.C. 28741; 704-526-2171. A mountain resort inn on Rtes. 28 & 64, 60 mi. from Ashville. Located in the heart of the Nantahala National Forest. Lodgings. American Plan. Breakfast, lunch and dinner served to travelers from May to November. Joan and Dick Lee, Innkeepers.

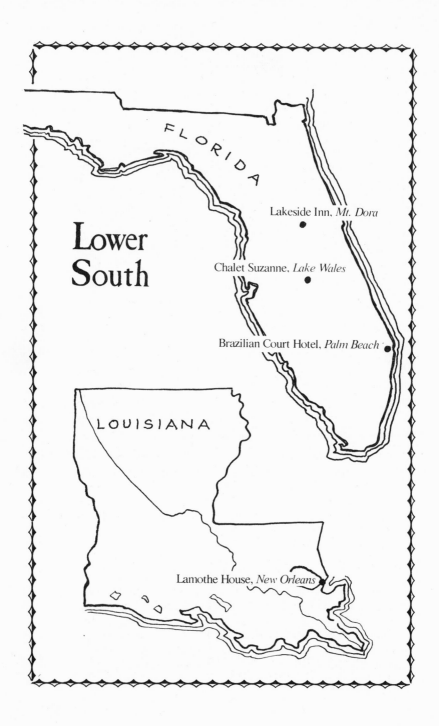

Lower
South

FLORIDA

Lakeside Inn, *Mt. Dora*

Chalet Suzanne, *Lake Wales*

Brazilian Court Hotel, *Palm Beach*

LOUISIANA

Lamothe House, *New Orleans*

Florida

For years I have been waiting for a clue to even one Florida country inn. This year, I found not one but three. The first is in the residential section of Palm Beach, the second two in central Florida, one at Lake Wales and the other northwest of Orlando in Florida's lake district at Mount Dora. On this particular trip I had little opportunity to do much backroading, but in the next edition I'm sure that there will be much to report on.

BRAZILIAN COURT HOTEL, Palm Beach

I found the *other* side of Palm Beach. Not the glittery, socialite side, but the face of Palm Beach that has real people. Furthermore, I was amazed to find a Palm Beach hotel with the simplicity and good taste that appeal to such people. It is called the Brazilian Court Hotel, although almost everyone refers to it as the BC.

The BC was built back in the 1920's, and the attractive residential area with sedate homes with beautifully landscaped gardens grew up around it. The building is a rather austere, two-story Palm Beach mission design, but oddly enough has penthouses. It is built around two completely enclosed patios. The first is a favorite place to catch the morning sun. It has several varieties of palm trees and flowers and pleasant arrangements of resort furniture.

I moved through the passageway flanked by two wrought iron staircases into the second patio, with a profusion of trees, flowers, bushes and plants. There is a very picturesque fountain in the middle. Dispersed around this enclosure are dining tables, many with umbrellas. Weather permitting, all three meals are served here, and each time of day has its own extremely captivating mood. There is also a glass enclosed main dining room used during the infrequent showers.

I believe this dining patio really sets the tone for this discreet hotel. For example, in the evening small lights twinkle on the inside of each of the umbrellas, and indirect colored lighting dramatically underscores the gorgeous palm trees and exotic tropical plants which abound. As the night grows darker the lights become more brilliant against the dark blue sky and there is a faint aura of unreality. Now add a three-piece orchestra playing lightly in the background and we have all of the elements of an intriguing ballet being played by a deft staff and the guests. It is quite reminiscent of the Black Point Inn at Prouts Neck and the Bethel Inn, both in Maine. It also resembles the Inn at Rancho Santa Fe, California.

Because there are many long-staying guests here, the selections on the menu are numerous and varied. The baked Pompano Almondine was mouth watering. My waiter was good enough to suggest that although rather simple, the macaroons for dessert would be an ideal touch of sweet. They were.

During a tour of the hotel the next morning with Innkeeper Bright Johnson, he pointed out that unlike other resort hotels the BC has no imposing main entrance. "It just wouldn't fit with what we are," he said. He's been at the hotel for 35 years and at almost every other step of the way he was stopping to exchange words of greeting with guests and introduced me to many of them. He pointed out to me that the BC was just two blocks from the ocean and that there is also a special sun deck atop one of the buildings. "For people who don't want to go down to the ocean every day to get a good tan," he said.

The lodging rooms and suites in the hotel are almost like my own living room and bedroom. The furniture has an "at home" quality. They were the kind of rooms in which I felt very comfortable. Instead of having hallways, groups of these rooms had their own entrance onto the patios.

I was delighted to find this genteel, well-mannered, small hotel in Palm Beach.

BRAZILIAN COURT HOTEL, 300 Brazilian Ave., Palm Beach, Fla. 33480; 305-655-7740. An intimate hotel in the heart of Palm Beach. 2 blocks from the ocean. Open mid-Dec. to early April. Lodgings on American and European Plan. Breakfast, lunch, dinner served to travelers. Bright Johnson, Innkeeper.

CHALET SUZANNE, Lake Wales

Where can I begin to describe the Chalet Suzanne? One place would be during the Great Depression of the '30's. At that time Bertha Hinshaw was a new widow with two children, $1,700 from a cancelled insurance policy, an old Studebaker and a Packard, a six-room house down a Florida dirt road about a mile from the main highway. She sold the cars, and decided to use the house as a restaurant. For ten days no one came. Then a family of five came and decided to stay for Christmas. Chalet Suzanne was off and running.

A fire in 1943 turned out to be a blessing because Bertha started all over again with some unique ideas about the designs of the buildings, and the Chalet Suzanne became famous not only for exceptional food, but for an atmosphere that looks like a set from a children's movie. There is a conglomoration of little lodges that simply defy description. It's Oriental, Bavarian, Swiss and Chocolate layer cake. There are little bridges, penthouses, steeples, cupolas, minaretes, peaked roofs, flat roofs, and little tiny windows from which I expected a veiled maiden to be peeking. There is even a Moorish dhow moored on the lake!

199

However, we are not through yet. Immediately adjacent to this wonderful, sugary, fairyland is a 2,600 ft. airstrip! This came as a result of Bertha's son, Carl's, interest in flying. In fact, he was so interested that he married a stewardess, Vita, and the two of them have been actively engaged in the management of the Chalet Suzanne during recent years. Carl, in addition to being a licensed pilot and instructor, is also the chef at the inn. Flyers from all over the country stop in for food and lodging.

Now, as if this wasn't enough, there is still another fascinating feature of this totally unusual country inn. About 13 years ago Carl and Vita realized that the guests were high in their praise of their Soup Romaine, so he and Vita decided to can it and make it available to the public. Today the Soup Factory is a thriving part of the whole Chalet Suzanne picture. I learned that it turns out 600,000 cans yearly, mostly to the gourmet sections of food and department stores. Incidentally, the Chalet Suzanne soups were taken on the Apollo 15 flight to the moon.

This is really a soupçon (I thought that was pretty clever) of the full story of Chalet Suzanne. I went there because it was recommended to me as a delightful country inn with exceptional food, and never in the world expected to find the rest of the story. For the next issue I've saved the stories about how Bertha collected most of the bric-a-brac, and how many well-known personalities have enjoyed themselves in the truly fantastic Victorian lodging rooms and restaurant overlooking the lake.

After Carl and Vita bade me goodby, I began to wonder whether it had all really happened, or was it like Brigadoon, a village that returns for one day every hundred years? I can hardly wait to go back the next time, to see if it's there.

CHALET SUZANNE, Lake Wales, Florida 33835; 813 676-1477. A phantasmagoric country inn and gourmet restaurant. 4½ mi. from Lake Wales with entrances on both U.S. Hgwy. 27 and 27A. Near Cypress Gardens and Disney World. Lodgings. European Plan. Dining room open from 8 a.m. to 9:30 p.m. daily. Closed Mondays from Labor Day to Memorial Day. The Hinshaw Family, Innkeepers.

LAKESIDE INN, Mount Dora

It was the first of March at the Lakeside Inn in Mount Dora. After breakfast the partings began. Many of the guests who had been here for one, two or even three months were leaving, and there were many exchanges of addresses, fervent handclasps, kisses and even a tear or two as the guests promised to keep in touch with one another until their return next year.

As Innkeeper Dick Edgerton explained, "The mornings on the first of the month are difficult and I hate to see them come. But it is wonderful to see many familiar faces arrive that same afternoon."

The entire community of Mount Dora is quite reminiscent of New England. The live oak trees are similar to the stately, but alas, disappearing New England elms. There are also quite a few homes similar to those in Canaan and Foxboro, built around lakes and low hills.

To add to the New England flavor, a great many of the inn's staff are employed at New England inns in the summertime, including the Black Point Inn. The resident manager, Mr. Harry Montague, was formerly the Superintendent of Schools in Brattleboro, Vermont, and another staff member, Cornelia Tarbell, runs the Old Stone Shop in Wallingford, Vermont in the summer.

But the Lakeside Inn belongs unquestionably to central Florida. It was still winter on the calendar, but the breezes were balmy. It was pleasantly cool in the morning, but by ten o'clock I was happy to shed my sweater and enjoy temperatures that would almost reach 80 degrees. Then, the inn pool was most welcome and quite a few other guests gathered, many of whom had earlier been playing golf at the nearby Mount Dora Country Club, antiquing, visiting Disney World, fishing, playing shuffleboard in the town square, sitting in on auctions, or lawn bowling.

Lawn bowling—now there is something interesting. Some of the inns in this book have lawn bowling courts, but the Mount Dora Lawn Bowling Club, just a few paces from the inn, is the most impressive I have ever seen. It was fun seeing so many people outdoors and obviously having such a good time. I'd like to try it sometime, but they all looked too good for a beginner!

I enjoyed myself meeting the guests of the inn, who, for the most part, were grandfathers and grandmothers. They were into everything. One woman took me around the inn grounds and named every flower, bush and tree, and gave me a short lecture on the ducks, cranes and flamingos. I had conversations with one or two retired professors, business executives, and an author or two. And talk about bridge players!

"We think there is no place like Mount Dora," said my botanical friend who has been returning for the past 15 years. "In fact, we come here at Christmas to escape our grandchildren. They are just too much." Several people, rocking on the long porch, joined in a chorus of agreement at that remark.

The Lakeside Inn is a lively resort-inn for involved, mature individuals. I was favorably impressed with the staff, the pleasant accommodations, and especially by the very happy times the guests and staff seemed to be enjoying with each other. I think Marie Edgerton summed it up very well: "It's an extension of our own home."

LAKESIDE INN, Mount Dora, Fla. 32757; 904-383-2151. A resort-inn on Lake Dora in central Florida about 45 min. northwest of Orlando on Rte. 441. Lodgings on American Plan only. Breakfast, lunch, dinner served to travelers. Open from December 15 — April 8. Richard Edgerton, Innkeeper.

Louisiana

I'm going to have a lot of fun in future years doing some of the back roads all around New Orleans. For one thing, this beautiful country abounds in historic mansions that have been painstakingly restored. Unfortunately, on my first trip I could visit only a relatively few places outside of the city. However, Mrs. Gertrude Munson is already planning the itinerary for my next trip, which will include many bayou country plantations and houses.

LAMOTHE HOUSE, New Orleans

Gertrude Munson and I were seated in the flagstone courtyard of the Lamothe House with its palms, magnolias, and gloriously-scented sweet olive trees. The hustle and bustle of the French Quarter seemed centuries away in this romantic patio and garden. She waved gaily to some guests who were walking around the second floor balcony to reach their room.

"The Lamothe House," she explained, "was built by two brothers from San Domingo when they fled here from a slave uprising. They established a sugar plantation near New Orleans, and built this town house in 1800 in almost complete duplicate. It has the same floor plans on both sides of the center hall, which divides the three floors of the house completely in half. We've converted the old formal parlors on the first floor into handsome suites with

elegant antique furnishings. I'm sure you noticed that
there are two lovely winding staircases going up to the
upper floors. The Lamothe brothers lived in this house for
many years until the War between the States, enjoying
all that New Orleans had to offer in the way of delightful
music and art and entertainment."

Some new guests walked in to inquire of Mrs. Munson about where they should spend the day in New
Orleans. Well they may, because she is a veritable fountain of information about everything historical and gas-
tronomic in this most unusual city. I had met them
earlier at "petit dejeuner" which is served in the elegant
dining room every morning from 8 a.m. to 10 a.m. with
Mrs. Munson pouring coffee from a two-hundred-year old,
handsome Sheffield urn, and providing charming and pro-
vocative conversation. Everyone was introduced, and
quite a few couples who were strangers before were now
planning to spend an enjoyable day in New Orleans together.

The Lamothe House has fourteen extremely pleasant
rooms, many with four-poster beds. Although it is a 19th
century restored mansion, every room is blessedly air
conditioned. When I was there in November the weather
was well nigh perfect. It is most necessary to reserve well
in advance.

I am most indebted to my friend, Jim Mellow of St. Louis, who taking his cue from the fact that we had included the Algonquin Hotel in New York in "Country Inns and Back Roads" suggested that the Lamothe House possessed all the characteristics of a country inn. He was right; it was all that I had hoped for, and even more.

LAMOTHE HOUSE, 621 Esplanade Ave., New Orleans, La. 70116; 504-947-1161. A small elegant inn in the French Quarter within walking distance of many fascinating New Orleans restaurants and attractions. Lodgings. Mod. American Plan, Continental breakfast, no other meals served. Open Sept. 1 — May 31. Mrs. Gertrude Munson, Innkeeper.

LOUISIANA — Early Beginnings

The early history of Louisiana is a little cloudy. The mouth of the Mississippi may have been discovered by Alonso de Pinneda in 1519. Probably Hernando de Soto entered the present State of Louisiana, and was buried there, but there is no proof of that. At any rate, Spain did not claim the region, and when la Salle came down the river in 1682 he took possession in the name of France.

In 1699, Pierre le Moyne d'Iberville made the first settlement, a fort about forty miles above the mouth of the Mississippi. This settlement did not prosper until John Law, the Scottish gambler and financier, got control of the colony. In 1718, New Orleans was founded and the settlers began to grow cotton in 1740, sugar cane in 1751.

However, in 1762, King Louis XV ceded all the territory of Louisiana to his cousin, the King of Spain. The colonists did not care to be ruled by Spain. In 1768 they attempted a revolt which was unsuccessful.

After 1765, hundreds of French exiles from Nova Scotia made their way to Louisiana. Descendants of these Acadians, known as "Cajuns" still live there.

The Farmhouse, *Port Townsend*
Captain Whidbey's, *Coupeville*

WASHINGTON

Heritage House, *Little River*

Sutter Creek Inn, *Sutter Creek*

Normandy Inn, *Carmel*

San Ysidro Ranch, *Santa Barbara*

Ojai Valley Inn, *Ojai*

The Inn, *Rancho Santa Fe*

FORNIA

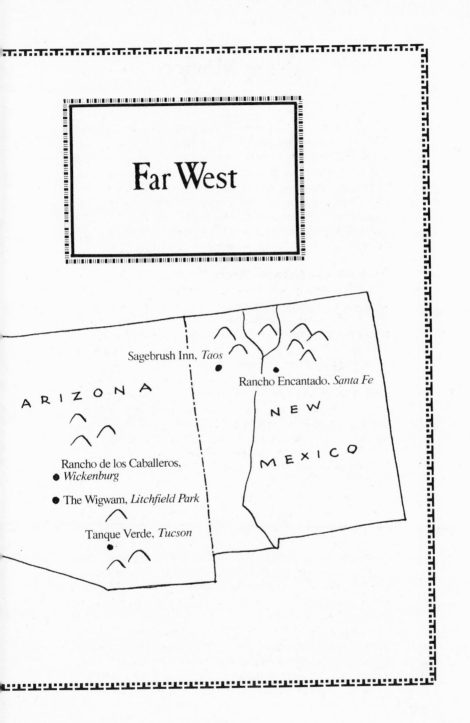

Far West

Sagebrush Inn, *Taos*

Rancho Encantado, *Santa Fe*

A R I Z O N A

N E W

M E X I C O

Rancho de los Caballeros,
Wickenburg

The Wigwam, *Litchfield Park*

Tanque Verde, *Tucson*

New Mexico

I guess with New Mexico you either do, or you don't like it. As someone once said, "Beauty is in the eye of the beholder." There may be more to life than majestic mountain ranges stretching away into the distance, clear blue skies, and rolling land dotted by bushes and trees. However, many people have come out here and found a way of life that meets their needs. Among these are Betty Egan of Rancho Encantado in Santa Fe, and Myron and Muriel Vallier of the Sagebrush Inn in Taos.

RANCHO ENCANTADO, Santa Fe

The morning sun streamed into my window, made even more brilliant by a new fallen snow of about four inches. It was February and the high chapparel had a wondrous coating of white with a back-lighting of azure blue skies. I was glad to have a fire laid in my bedroom to take the chill off the morning.

From my window and patio I could see the swimming pool which would be active in just a few more months and the corral which, among other things, has a huge buffalo on view. It would be the starting point that morning for a trail ride on the desert. The tennis courts were also covered with the white stuff, but in my imagination I could hear the ping of raquet on ball in a few more weeks, for there is activity the year 'round.

One of the things that appeals to me about this mountain-ringed ranch-inn is the fact that the guests' privacy is protected. For example, a governor from a large eastern state spent quite a bit of time here recently without the world outside really knowing where he was. This is also true of other well-known guests from the entertainment world and politics. In many ways it is like the Hotel Algonquin in New York where busy people may relax and be themselves.

The spirit and inspiration of Rancho Encantado is Betty Egan, whose good taste, perseverance and courage launched this resort inn a few years ago against what seemed to be insurmountable odds. Now it is a success,

and probably more important to her, she is an important part of the local community which is known as Tesuque (pronounced Tee-SOO-key). In fact, she is active in everything that will enable the environment and ecology to be protected. Foremost among her enthusiasm is the fact that she is the only lady fire chief in New Mexico! She looks adorable in the helmet.

I very much enjoyed my first visit to Rancho Encantado a year earlier, but this time I could see it in a much broader sense. Although it is a luxury ranch-inn, it is also a meeting place for many of the permanent residents of the community, and for two nights I sat in the handsome living room well past my bedtime discussing local problems such as schools, clean water, and land development, which seem to be rife wherever I travel. The concern in this area is heightened perhaps by the fact that there is a merging of three cultures, Indian, Spanish and Anglo.

My reverie was broken by the arrival of my room service breakfast, which in a warmer month would be served on my own private patio. What a way to begin the day!

RANCHO ENCANTADO, Rte. 4, Box 57C, Santa Fe, N.M.. 87501; 505-982-3537. A luxurious ranch-inn a few miles northwest of Santa Fe, off Rte. 285 at Tesuque. Lodgings. European Plan. Breakfast, lunch, dinner served for travelers. Open all year. Betty Egan, Innkeeper.

SAGEBRUSH INN, Taos

Myron and Muriel Vallier are from New Hampshire, and the Sagebrush Inn in Taos is about as New England a country inn as I'll ever find in New Mexico. The big difference, of course, is that the architecture is Spanish colonial. The building and the lodging rooms are all built of adobe brick, and the rugs, wall hangings, lamps, doors, door latches, and the entire feeling, is unquestionably New Mexican.

Here I was in the beautiful lobby. All around me was comfortable furniture inviting anyone to stop and rest and talk with others. Some of the leather back chairs have original designs painted on them. The walls are decorated with paintings of the local Taos artists. There is a generous amount of Indian pottery and Indian crafts. The great massive ceiling is supported by huge vigas and planks in keeping with the local architecture. The room looked very relaxing and comfortable and, as I later discovered, is extremely well used by the house guests.

The lobby leads out to portals which surround the patios off of which the lodging rooms have been built. There is a profusion of flowers, birds and bushes. One of the lodging rooms is three stories high in the pueblo-like building and has windows on four sides. It is a kind of watch tower, and I was told it was one of the most sought after rooms in the inn.

The food at the Sagebrush Inn is hearty, and for the most part, southwestern. There is a great deal of emphasis on various kinds of beef as well as native foods, such as a special chalupa which is made from homemade tortillas, refritos, green chilies in tomato sauce, and guacamole. There are enchiladas, chili rellenos and huevos rancheros. The Sagebrush Inn is known for its Saturday night buffet.

Interestingly enough, it was the breakfast at the Sagebrush Inn which first brought the inn to my attention. While I was dining at Rancho Encantado, one of the guests mentioned that when skiing at Taos Valley he tried to leave early in the morning so that he could get one of those breakfasts which were, in his words, "terrific." This breakfast includes fried ham, fried potatoes, fresh chilies, scrambled eggs, and green chili omelets with bacon slices.

In the lobby of the Sagebrush Inn one large window has a perfect view of Taos Mountain which can be seen at all hours of the day and night with all of its changing complexion and beauty. It is close to the Taos Indian Pueblo, the first multi-story dwelling in America, built about 700 years ago.

The town of Taos is a very picturesque place steeped in traditions and legends from its founding in 1615. Today it is one of the foremost art colonies in the country. Recreation is varied here in the high mountains of New Mexico and includes fishing, hunting, horseback riding, winter skiing, and the fun of exploring the many mountain trails, ghost towns and old Spanish villages — all within a very reasonable distance.

The Sagebrush Inn is bright, cheerful, friendly and homey. Many people have been coming back year after year to visit the Valliers. It is advisable during the summer season to have reservations booked considerably in advance.

SAGEBRUSH INN, P.O. Box 1566, Taos, N.M. 87571; 505-758-2254. A New Mexican country inn on Rte. 64, 2 mi. south of Taos (Santa Fe Rd.), in the heart of the Sangre de Christo Mts. Lodgings. European Plan. Breakfast, dinner served daily with buffet on Sat. evening. Alpine ski. Myron and Muriel Vallier, Innkeepers.

Arizona

By now, Arizona is beginning to look like a second home to us. The ranch-inns in Wickenburg and Tucson provide a highly unique vacation as well as the golf-resort inn in Litchfield Park.

THE WIGWAM, Litchfield Park

He had that distinguished, well-tanned look, with a touch of silver at the temples. I thought: "He looks like Walter Pidgeon." We were sitting around the pool in the full mid-afternoon Arizona sunshine. The deck chairs were rapidly filling with a genial, informal group, and there was talk of "birdies and pars and sandtraps and bunkers." It seemed impossible that only the previous day I had dug my car out of a foot of snow, a thousand miles to the north. "Where," I asked myself, "have I been, when I could have been playing golf, riding on the desert, getting a tan and living like visiting royalty here?"

A gentleman came out of the water, picked-up one of the huge, colorful pool towels and said: "First day here I see, watch that sun, the southwest air is so clear that you'll have plenty of color very quickly.

"Golf's the big thing here," he said. "There are two golf courses, both beautiful. One is 7220 yds. from the back tees with a par 72, and the other is 6172 yds. and a par 70. Today I played them both. You know, Robert Trent Jones designed them, and he certainly knows how to build a golf course."

"I'll tell you something else though, tennis is really catching on in a big way down here. Do you know that they have 8 new courts in now, and you can play on six of them at night. They also have a very good teaching program which is particularly good for the young people.

"We came down from Minneapolis last week and I think the pro has taken three strokes off my game already. We were here over the Thanksgiving holiday last year, and this year we're having my son and his family come down during the Easter holidays and bring the kids."

I have been asked several times why I have included the Wigwam for the last few years in a book about coun-

try inns. It is, in fact, rather large, although this is a country where things are done in a big way! However, I think one of the keys for me is the fact that Reade White-well, the innkeeper, and his staff still maintain a very personal contact with most of the guests. To an Easterner, this whole manner of southwest living is something new. Each time I go out for a visit I am glad I threw away the rule book, and from the letters and comments I have received from my readers I think they are too.

THE WIGWAM, Litchfield Park, Ariz. 85340; 602-935-3811. A luxury resort-inn with two Robert Trent Jones golf courses. 17 miles from Phoenix. American Plan. Breakfast, lunch and dinner served to travelers daily. Open early October to late May. Reade Whitewell, Innkeeper.

TANQUE VERDE, Tucson

The postmark on the letter said "Caldwell, New Jersey." It said in part: "We've been reading about your last visit to the Tanque Verde Ranch just outside of Tucson. It sounds very intriguing. My wife and I are enthusiastic about the prospect of a new vacation experience in the desert country. The idea of staying at a ranch that may have even survived Indian raids, and your descriptions of steak over mesquite fires, and bird-watching, are most inviting. However, it is a long way for us to go, and neither of us have ever been astride a horse. We're both about fifty years old and we'd like a little more advice as to whether we should venture forth on this trip."

Until about three years ago, horseback riding for me consisted of a couple short hauls on a Tennessee walking horse and one or two rides on the gentlest nag in my local livery stable. When I went out to Tanque Verde the first time I talked this over with Sam, the head wrangler, and

213

he picked out a horse that he thought was the right size for my weight and had enough experience to guide me.

On that first ride there were a husband and wife from the Boston area, who were at a western ranch for  the first time and who were on their first morning trail ride. We took off out of the corral in single file into the desert, and the entire experience was so exhilarating that by the time we got back to the ranch my Massachusetts neighbors were inquiring of Sam as to whether they could have more active horses, and if they could go for a longer ride the next day. Sam looked very wise and said, "I think I'd wait and see how you feel after today's ride."

Of course he was right, although the whirlpool baths took care of the aches! By the end of the week these people had purchased some blue jeans, ranch type shirts, cowboy hats, and boots and knew all the horses by their first names.

At Tanque Verde I discovered a completely different type of vacation. It is simply impossible to be isolated unless you want to spend the entire time in one of those attractive casitas reading a book, or at the pool. I can't imagine anyone being there for more than two days without having made at least six to ten new friends. As for children, they take to ranch life like a duck to water!

I'm very anxious to hear how my correspondents from New Jersey enjoyed their stay at the Tanque Verde.

TANQUE VERDE RANCH, Box 515, Rte. 8, Tuscon, Ariz. 85710; 602-296-6275. A ranch-inn on East Speedway Rd. American Plan. All facilities for a complete ranch vacation. Meals served to travelers by reservation. Open all year. Robert Cote, Innkeeper.

RANCHO DE LOS CABALLEROS, Wickenburg

Vulture Peak was behind us now. From our raised elevation, the valley stretched out in a splendid panorama clear across to the Weavers and the Bradshaws, distant blue mountains seemingly so close in the clear Wickenburg air. Spread below us, about three quarters of an hour away on our gentle-paced steeds, were the adobe bungalows, the sprawling ranch-style main house, the tennis courts, the corrals, and sapphire blue oval of the swimming pool. This was Rancho de los Caballeros!

Everywhere I went in southern Arizona — from innkeepers and owners of other guest ranches — I heard: "Be sure and see los Caballeros."

Picking up the call of home, the horses quickened their speed. The trail led down through the beautiful high desert with the cactus showing signs of early bloom. We passed the grazing ranch cattle and flushed out a pair of jackrabbits.

From the conversations I had had the previous evening, I already knew that the other adult guests were most enthusiastic about "los Caballeros" — it's food, accommodations and beauty. I wondered how the younger generation felt and leaned forward to speak to my new partner and riding companion, twelve year old Jimmy:

"Do you like it here?"

"Oh, boy, I'll say I do. I wish I could live here all the time. My brother and I get to ride horses everyday, and then we meet with the lady in that big tepee next to the swimming pool, and we all go hiking in the geode field, have treasure hunts, and visit the gold mine. We also get to follow the chuck wagon out into the desert and have some of our meals, too. One of the big things is to visit the London Bridge, and the real ghost town, too. Excuse me now, I've got to ride ahead and talk with Tommy, the head wrangler."

He paused for just a minute and lowered his voice: "There's just one thing. Try to remember to sit tall in the saddle."

RANCHO DE LOS CABALLEROS, Wickenburg, Ariz. 85338; 602-684-5484. A luxury ranch-inn about 60 mi. north of Phoenix on Rte. 60 in the high desert. American Plan. Breakfast, lunch, dinner served to travelers. Open mid-October to early May. Mr. Dallas Gant, Jr., Innkeeper.

California

There are a few changes in our California inns in this edition. The constant reader may note that a few from our previous editions have been omitted, however, there are two new inns. One is on the coast of southern California in the Montecito section of Santa Barbara. The other is just north of San Diego at Rancho Santa Fe. California is a great state for back roading. In fact, some of the principal roads are spectacular. For example, the Redwood Highway, 101, north of Leggett through the big tree country is breathtaking. There are also some real back roads off Route 49 going east into the mountains.

THE INN, Rancho Santa Fe

The two towering eucalyptus trees were benign sentinels on the path that led from the front entrance of The Inn straight down to the village of Rancho Santa Fe. On either side of the broad front lawn, one side of which had a lawn bowling green, were two of the many rambling cottages which have been covertly placed among the spacious trees, lawns and gardens. The evening sky was the deepest blue, and stars were twinkling diamonds. No smog here. Discreet floodlighting accented the myriad shapes.

I was enchanted with the fragrances of Southern California. On this balmy, sub-tropical night, I couldn't possibly single out one from the dozen of varieties wafting from the vegetation.

It is impossible to consider The Inn without becoming involved in the concept of Rancho Santa Fe itself. It has been described as a *civilized planned community* where the homes and estates have been created in perfect harmony with nature's generous endowment of climate and scenery.

For one thing, the town fathers take an extremely hard line on the subject of anything which will in any way detract from the natural beauty of the area. As an example, a local ordinance states that no home garages may be built with an entrance facing the street! Innkeeper Steve Royce, who was most courteous and patient about giving me a complete tour of Rancho Santa Fe, explained that everything is under strict zoning and architectural control.

In such a setting, nothing less than a paragon of all country inns would be appropriate. The Inn is a wonderfully elegant little place with such unusual touches as triple sheets, turn-down service and real fireplaces blazing in the lobby and many of the rooms. At the same time, it is very warm and informal with great appeal to guests who enjoy outdoor living.

There are golf privileges available at one of the three nearby private country clubs, tennis and swimming on the inn's grounds and ocean swimming at nearby Del Mar beach where the inn has its own beach cottage. I was delighted also with the 4,000 book library.

In addition to the picturesque surroundings, the inn's location makes it a natural starting point for the unusual in sightseeing in California including Old Mexico, just an hour's drive away.

Steve Royce, who is well known as the former owner of the Huntington Hotel in Pasadena, makes it a point to visit with each guest at some time during their stay. He has an unending supply of anecdotes and stories from his life in the hotel business. But what is probably even more unique, the inn is still a family run operation with Steve's daughter, niece, son-in-law and son Danny, the third generation of the family to have followed in the hotel business, all contributing their share to the daily operation and charm.

Just imagine what a delight this gentle, warm, fragrant discovery in Southern California meant to a frostbitten New Englander! I was told that it was an Elysium, but this description falls considerably short for Rancho Santa Fe.

THE INN, Rancho Santa Fe, Calif. 92067; 714-756-1131. A resort-inn 27 mi. north of San Diego, via San Diego Freeway #5, and 5 mi. inland from Solana Beach, Del Mar. Coming from either the north or the south on Freeway #5, take the Lomas Santa Fe turn-off. Lodgings. Breakfast, lunch and dinner served daily to travelers. Open all year. Stephen Royce, Innkeeper.

OJAI VALLEY INN, Ojai

It was that kind of a morning — a little past 8 o'clock. The putting green had already been swept free of the dew and the smog-free air was so clear and dry that I felt as though I could drive every green on the course, or serve an ace with every attempt. It was late February in Ojai, but this is Spring in Southern California. The robins were nested in the oak trees, the plantings on the patio were in early bloom, and the fairways and greens looked beautiful to me, as my own golf course was under eight inches of snow!

I envied the couple who appeared to be the first people to tee-off this morning. They were in for a beautiful day. Not that it means anything I suppose, but she

did out-drive him off the first tee. I wondered how they would be doing at the 18th green.

The Ojai Valley Inn is a place for alert, active, outdoor-loving people to enjoy themselves. The tennis program has been aided by the addition of new tennis courts since my last visit, and the little swimming pool, from whence I called home last year during a New England blizzard, is still a jewel. The mountains that ring the community of Ojai invite horseback trail rides and the inn has stables with several good mounts available, and guides who know the territory.

The inn is an interesting combination of Spanish Mission architecture blended with old English prints and even a copper bas-relief of William Shakespeare over the fireplace in the living room. It is surrounded by beautiful live oaks, evergreens, eucalyptus, and an occasional palm tree. There is a profusion of birds who find it easy to nest among the curved roof tiles. Innkeeper Bill Briggs tells me that they are also under the American Plan!

Because the accent is on outdoor living here, the focal point seems to be the patio where lunch is served every day. Some of my most pleasant memories of visits here are of sitting underneath the spreading branches of the tree, with all of the guests dressed in gay California colors. We are able to watch the action on the 18th green as well as three tees at the same time.

This time my lodging room had one complete wall of glass and when I pulled the curtains in the morning there was the panorama of the mountains, ascending level by level, before me. Incidentally, this inn is another place where the beds are turned down each evening.

Another golfing couple stopped and told me they were unable to contain themselves any longer. They had been watching me with the tape recorder wandering around the grounds and asked what I was doing. When I explained, they became enthusiastic boosters for the inn: "Oh, this is really one of our favorite places. It isn't that far from Los Angeles and we always meet nice people when we come here. Some of them don't even play golf, or tennis, or horseback ride — they just enjoy the sunshine and the friendships that they make."

It is observations like this that convince me that while country inns certainly mean clean lodgings, good food, and frequently some very interesting activity, the most important factor is really people. At the Ojai Valley Inn I am always meeting beautiful people.

OJAI VALLEY INN & COUNTRY CLUB, Ojai, Calif. 93023; 805-646-5511. A resort-inn with its own championship golf course on U.S. 33, 19 mi. northeast of Ventura. Lodgings. American Plan. Breakfast, lunch, dinner served to travelers. Open all year. Bill Briggs, Innkeeper.

SAN YSIDRO RANCH, Santa Barbara

Innkeeper Maggi Carr and I were standing on the patio of the adobe office. "This is one of the oldest buildings in the Santa Barbara area," she asserted. "In 1964 it was dedicated as a historical monument. In many ways it preserves the tradition of the property. It has much memorabilia of the ranch's days one hundred years ago."

I learned that San Ysidro was established as a ranch by the padres of the Santa Barbara Mission in 1780. It came into private ownership just before the turn of the last century and became a guest ranch in the 1890's.

Maggi and I walked through the gardens and citrus orchards, past the tennis courts, to the swimming pool. Every few feet along the way, I was aware of a different aroma. The trees were all a-twitter with birds.

Along the way we looked in on a few of the white cottages which comprise the lodgings. All have been beautifully landscaped and most have fireplaces. Mine also happened to be next to the creek which rushes down

from the canyon, and because there was no television or radio, I could hear all of the fascinating natural sounds of southern California, particularly in the early morning hours.

As we approached the pool, I nudged Maggi and said, "Isn't that what's-his-name, the jogging governor?"

"Yes, that's right. This is his little hideaway. As a matter of fact, quite a few people from both the political and entertainment fields are here frequently. Prince Adaboe of Nigeria is here this week. Ronald Coleman was once co-owner. Perhaps you noticed his bust on display next to a few of the old registers?"

Yes, I had noticed those registers, and among other names were the late President Kennedy and Jacqueline Kennedy when they honeymooned here. Also Winston Churchill, Somerset Maugham, and Katherine Hepburn visited here. Let me emphasize, however, that the San Ysidro is not a place where one comes to be seen. Rather, it is a place where one comes to be one's self.

The Santa Inez Mountains provide some first rate riding trails, and the whole area is bathed in that fabulous southern California sunshine. I did manage to get in a few sets of tennis while I was there, although the golf had to be postponed until a later visit. There is a private beach on the Santa Barbara Bay for swimming and surfing.

Yes, long gone are the days of the Dons. Elegant vaqueros and senoritas have given way to the casually-garbed guests of today. However, it is the same beautiful part of California which the Spaniards loved and deeply cherished. And fortunately much of that quietude has been preserved. Montecito, itself, is one of the picturebook communities of California, and because the ranch was here first, the elegantly designed homes have grown up around it.

John Galsworthy, the English writer, was a guest here in the early 1920's. Here is an excerpt from something he wrote about San Ysidro:

"How beautiful! The loveliness of these evenings moves the heart; and of the mornings, shining, cool, fragrant."

It may well be that Ronald Coleman, moved by the experience of playing in "Lost Horizons," may have seen in San Ysidro some of that elusive Shangri-la quality that Galsworthy also sensed.

SAN YSIDRO RANCH, Montecito, Santa Barbara, Calif. 93108; 805-969-5046. A luxurious ranch-inn in the Santa Inez Mountains (Exit San Ysidro Rd. off U.S. 101, Montecito, follow San Ysidro Rd. and Lane.) Lodgings. European Plan. Breakfast and dinner served to travelers daily. Lunch on Sat. and Sun. Maggi Carr, Innkeeper.

NORMANDY INN, Carmel

It was the 25th of February, but to me it felt like June 25th back in the Berkshires. The Carmel sun was so warm that I was sitting in my shirt sleeves, and the swimming pool in the garden at the Normandy Inn was most inviting. It was very quiet and tranquil. Bougainvillea and other flowers were already in bloom, and I noted a great number of potted flowers placed very strategically among the various walks and terraces of the garden. My reflections were interrupted by the arrival of a woman in a bathing suit.

"This inn reminds me of an inn I stayed in in Northern France," she said. "It's the series of outside galleries, wooden stairs and that marvelous courtyard. There seems to be no end of little passages between buildings. Don't you just love it here?"

I agreed readily. Not to be outdone, I asked her if she had seen the Breakfast Room as yet.

"We just arrived at noon, but I peeked as we were coming in. I understand that they have the most marvelous fresh rolls and buns each morning, along with orange juice and coffee."

I asked her which kind of room she was in, and she replied that she had one with a fireplace and kitchen.

"It's just sort of old-fashioned European," she asserted, "everything is so neat. We've a little cottage in the garden across the road."

Her son, a young lad about ten, came in and after we were introduced I asked him what he was going to do for the afternoon. "Oh, we're going to Point Lobos, and see if we can watch the sea otters. Tomorrow we're going to drive down to Big Sur and then we're going to some kind of castle down that way, too." His mother parenthetically explained: "The Hearst Castle at San Simeon."

Innkeeper Mike Stanton, I believe, put his finger right on what the Normandy Inn is really all about. "We think of it as an environment," he said. "My father is the architect and my mother is the decorator, and it definitely reflects their ideas about living. For example, we change all of these potted flowers twelve times a year, and up in the Breakfast Room we change the flowers and the candles, the placemats and even the slipcovers according to the different seasonal emphasis."

In talking with Mike, I discovered that from January through April, and from October through Christmas are the really exceptional times of the year to visit Carmel. "It's more leisurely," he said, "and certainly the weather is the greatest . . . just look at today."

I assuredly couldn't fault him on that.

NORMANDY INN, Carmel, Cal. 93921; 408-624-3825. Ocean Ave. between Monteverde and Casanova. A French Provincial inn in the heart of Carmel, within walking distance of beach, shops, restaurants, etc. Lodgings; Continental Plan (light breakfast); no other meals Mike Stanton, Innkeeper.

SUTTER CREEK INN, Sutter Creek

My, things had certainly changed over the past few years since my first visit to Jane Way at the Sutter Creek Inn. The basic New Hampshire farmhouse still looked the same, the grapevines, draped over the arbor where breakfast is served in the warm weather, had become fuller, and if anything, there seemed to be a more than usual quota of birds flitting about on this bright morning. But, these are the things that will never change. What has changed is the number of rooms and the number of guests stopping at the inn.

I recall that when I first came here there were about six rooms. Now, with the addition of outbuildings and new wings, there are a total of sixteen rooms, each of them furnished individually. In looking over the list I was surprised at the number that had fireplaces, or as in one case, an old Franklin stove. For instance, on this trip my room on the second floor in the front of the inn had a double bed and I shared a bathroom with another room. The bathtub was big enough for me to almost stretch out in it completely. On an earlier visit I had stayed in what was called the "Upper Wash House" which has a double and a single bed and its own full bath. The lodgings have interesting names such as Miner's Cabin, Payday House, Tool Shed, Woodshed Room and Lindsay's Room.

Lindsay, in this particular case, is Jane's young daughter, home again after accomplishments in the world of academe and very much interested in not only the inn, but in the ecology of the great gold rush district. As she and I were walking up the village street, she was saying: "I think we do have one of the best preserved 19th century environments in the gold country. You see, the local

merchants have made an effort to preserve something of
the history of the town, placing large posters in their
windows with anecdotes and information about Sutter
Creek of 100 years or more ago. At a time when everyone
is torn between the past and the realities of the future,
I think our business men have done a very good job. We
are all trying to preserve the outer approaches to Sutter
Creek, as well. The beautiful grazing lands and farms
make this section a great deal like New England. Don't
you agree?"

I do, indeed, agree. I think that Sutter Creek and the
area around it is quite similar to communities of inland
New England. One of the guests at the big family-style
breakfast served at the inn every morning at 9 a.m. sharp
remarked that she thought that the gold rush country was
very close to being like Vermont, and in a great many
ways it is.

The Sutter Creek Inn is a small, intimate, adult inn.
Lodgings include the hot breakfast. It is a very warm,
accommodating, antique-decorated, personal experience,
and many of the guests return again and again.

This morning I sat in the front living room where it
was so quiet I could hear the Grandfather clock ticking.
The big calico cat gingerly made his way across the chess
table without disturbing a single piece, and on soft pad-
ded feet negotiated the partially finished jigsaw puzzle.
He plumped down next to me. I asked him whether or
not he objected to the fact that young children were really

not welcome here because the inn was too small. He just snuggled a little closer and purred a little deeper.

SUTTER CREEK INN, 75 Main St., Sutter Creek, Calif. 95685; 209-267-5606. A village inn on the main street of historic Mother Lode town. 35 mi. from Sacramento on Hgwy. 49. Lodgings. Mod. American Plan includes a hot breakfast. Closed first two weeks in Jan. Mrs. Jane Way, Innkeeper.

HERITAGE HOUSE, Little River

It might have been the Maine Coast. The sixty-foot cliffs looked out over an ocean disarmingly calm. The sloping lawn led back up to an ivy-covered white Colonial that could have graced Kennebunkport. Behind it was a low hill covered with evergreens that reminded me of Bar Harbor. Taken all together, the guest houses looked like a village scene near Bucksport, seventy-five years ago. Even the names had the flavor: "Firehouse," "Schoolhouse," "Chart Room," "Ice Cream Parlor," "Apple House," "Barber Pole," and "Stable."

However, I was sitting in a rustic chair on the edge of the Pacific at Heritage House in Little River, California.

"There's good reason for you to feel like you're in Maine," explained Innkeeper Don Dennen. "Many 'down easters' came out here over one hundred years ago, lured by the big timber. Naturally, the homes they built were similar to those they left behind. There are many along the Mendicino coast."

The guest houses were inspired by old early-day buildings. Mine was the "Country Store," and like most of the others it had many antiques and its own fireplace. There were a few with sod roofs, something I've never seen in New England.

The New England influence is very strong in this lovely little seaside inn. However, I believe the Dennens have blended the best of both coasts, because there is a reaching out for new ideas, a willingness to try new things that is typical of California.

This is reflected in the menu and the service as well. To illustrate: This is the only place where I've had corned beef spiced with ginger; or where I was asked how crisp I wanted breakfast bacon, and where I could make my own toast at my breakfast table. Meanwhile, through a very clever communications system, my bed was being made and the room freshened up. "We think that guests should return to a civilized-looking room," Don explained. Later, there is a complete cleaning.

Guest cottage

From San Francisco, 140 miles away, I believe the fastest way to Little River is via Rte. 101 to Cloverdale. The Coastal Highway #1 through Bodega Bay, Jenner and Point Arena sometimes seems to hang by its fingernails on the cliffs over the ocean. It takes about 45 minutes longer.

HERITAGE HOUSE, Little River, Cal. 95456; 707-937-5885. An elegant oceanside inn on Coast Highway # 1, 144 mi. north of San Francisco. Mod. American Plan (omits lunch). Breakfast and dinner served by reservation. Closed Dec., Jan. Don Dennen, Innkeeper.

Washington

It was the first time in the northwest for me and thanks to Joan White and Wyn and Kathy Wright, I have been thoroughly innoculated with Seattle fever. In spite of all the rumors about the weather, my weekend there in February was sunny and pleasant for the most part.

There are two striking things about Seattle. One is the fact that there are literally hundreds of miles of waterways which are traversed by clean, prompt, convenient ferries. The other are the snowcapped mountain ranges on both sides. I found two country inns on this trip and will be returning in September in search of still more.

THE CAPTAIN WHIDBEY, Coupeville

"Welcome to The Captain Whidbey." Kathy Wright and I both turned around instantly, and there he was — complete with tweeds, snow white hair, corn cob pipe and a marvelous flat accent — Stephen Stone, a Nantucketeer if I ever saw and heard one. It was the last thing I expected to see here in Coupeville, Washington 3,000 miles away from the "Gray Lady of the Sea."

I had seen a postcard of The Captain Whidbey which showed its rustic exterior and suggested the presence of water, but I was totally unprepared for the extensive collection of antiques, bric-a-brac, original oil paintings, pewter, silver, ship models, spinning wheels, books and memorabilia which greeted us inside.

Although it was a busy Saturday lunch, Steve and his wife, Shirlie, were able to join us, and it wasn't long before we found we had several friends in common, including David Wood, another Nantucketeer from nearby Lenox, whom I have known for many years.

We ate in the "Chart Room" which has a low ceiling, beautifully finished beams and a broad view of Penn Cove, which Steve explained was named for the original William Penn. Incidentally, I had my first taste of the world renowned Dungeness crab meat which was baked in a shell with butter and herbs. I sampled a bit of Kathy's Pacific Halibut steak. Excellent.

Steve and Shirlie explained that Coupeville is one of the oldest towns in Washington and that the inn was

built in 1907 of Madrona logs. It has been a family inn for most of the 60 years and has had surprisingly few innkeepers. The waitresses all wore gingham dresses, and Kathy pointed out the pistol handled knives. While we were lunching, a few power boats pulled up to the dock and people came in for lunch. One couple was staying for the night.

This quite naturally led to a tour of the lodging rooms on the second floor where the first things that greeted us were a huge wall of books, an old spinning wheel, a marble top music cabinet, and a long hall filled with all kinds of things to delight collectors. Most of this is from Steve and Shirlie's own collection.

Rooms in The Captain Whidbey do not have their own bathrooms, but they do share a common gentlemen's room and a ladies' room which include bath facilities. There are a few cottages that do have their own facilities.

The terrace facing the cove is surrounded with plantings of holly, Oregon grape, fir trees, Indian paintbrush, Scotch broom, English ivy, junipers and fig trees. I'm still puzzling over the Seattle area climate!

Shirlie said that they see whales in the waters of the cove now and then. "Some of them are a pretty good size, too," she said.

To round out the picture, we went back inside to a little shop where The Captain Whidbey old-fashioned biscuit mix and jam are sold, as well as a nice selection of country things. Steve introduced me to his son, John, who is a student at Western Washington State College and is going to join his father and mother in the innkeeping business.

At the end of the day, Shirlie and Steve bade us good-by, and we headed for the ferry once again. We both agreed that it was just the kind of an inn that should be included in "Country Inns and Back Roads."

THE CAPTAIN WHIDBEY, Coupeville, Wash. 98239; 206-678-4097. A country inn by the sea on the shore road from Coupeville to Oak Harbor. Whidbey Island is reached year 'round by the Columbia Beach-Mukilteo Ferry, and during the summer by the port Townsend-Keystone Ferry. Lodgings. European Plan. Breakfast, lunch, dinner served to travelers all year. Steve and Shirlie Stone, Innkeepers.

THE FARMHOUSE, Port Townsend

Life is a series of circles, isn't it? It is surprising how many people we meet again after many years of separation. For example, it was in Seattle, Washington that I had a reunion with my dear friend, Joan White, who at one time was the producer at the Berkshire Summer Theatre in Stockbridge. We did several plays together. Now she lives in Seattle and was kind enough to call our book, "Country Inns and Back Roads," to the attention of her associate in the drama department at the University of Washington, Mr. John Conway, who runs a fascinating restaurant called The Farmhouse.

Thus, on a beautiful Sunday in February, Joan and I, united after at least a five-year separation, were on the ferry from Seattle to the Olympic Peninsula and the shores of the Strait of Juan de Fuca at Port Townsend to visit this country restaurant.

I'm going to let John continue the story about The Farmhouse in his own words:

"We built a little Japanese house in Port Townsend where I could be an old man. Then Dorothy, my wife, saw a gorgeous tree near our property line and fell in love with it. It is a 150-year-old Sitka spruce. So we bought this house to get the tree, remodeled it and then wondered what we would do with it. Then Jim Beard came along and suggested that we open a restaurant.

"Starting in September, after the Labor Day weekend, we will go into our ethnic winter schedule in which we serve dinners only on Saturdays, Sundays and holidays. September will be devoted to Japanese food as we knew it during our stay in Japan, where I learned to cook in a geisha house. October will feature Tuscan and Sicilian food to celebrate Columbus' voyage to, if not his discovery of, the New World. November is Hungarian month including Szekeley gulyas. We do take time out for an American dinner on Thanksgiving Day. In December we serve Yorkshire food built around roast beef and Yorkshire pudding.

"On Christmas Day we have a traditional dinner beginning at 3 p.m., and also on New Year's Day. We are closed in January for three weeks to refurbish, rest and catch-up. We are open again the first weekend in February with Northern Chinese Imperial food. Weekends in

March we serve the food from Provence in southern France. April is the month for native Greek specialities, and in May we'll be celebrating Buddha's birthday with East Indian curries and Sambals.

John explained that during the summer schedule—June, July and August—Fridays emphasize the wonderful fish fresh from the nearby strait. "On Saturdays we have red meat such as standing rib roast, and on Sundays we cook fowl in many different ways. Our famous salad bar features 25 salads. Luncheons during the summer include fish, crab and oysters, plus a salad."

Visiting The Farmhouse was a great experience. In fact, I am inspired to return there in September of this year not only to visit further country inns in the Seattle area, but also to enjoy another exceptional meal with John and Dorothy. That would be the Japanese month.

All meals are by reservation only and the sittings are at six and nine o'clock. I can assure you that regardless of how long it takes to get there, or how many times you get lost, you will appreciate it.

THE FARMHOUSE, North Beach, Port Townsend, Wash. 98368; 206-385-1411. (Seattle ⚏: 206-LA3-4625.) No lodgings. All meals served by reservation only. Dinners only from Sept. through May on Saturdays and Sundays. (See above paragraphs for ethnic specialties.) Summer schedule—June, July, August: Dinners, Friday, Saturday and Sunday. Lunch on Saturday and Sunday. Most essential that reservations be made, and also directions to reach them. Dorothy and John Ashby Conway, Innkeepers.

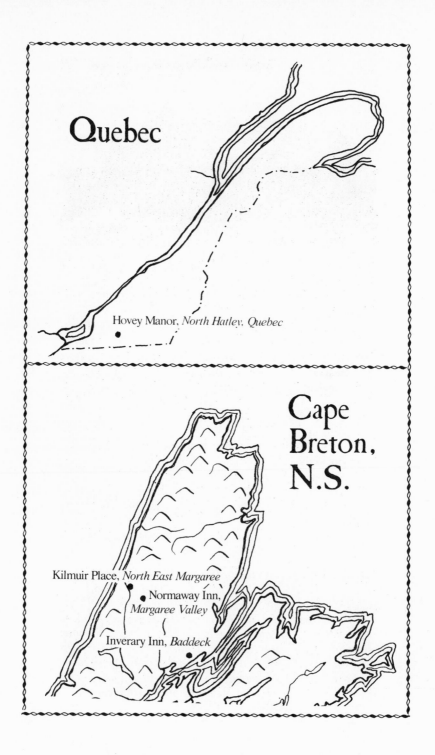

Quebec

Hovey Manor, *North Hatley, Quebec*

Cape Breton, N.S.

Kilmuir Place, *North East Margaree*

Normaway Inn, *Margaree Valley*

Inverary Inn, *Baddeck*

Quebec

I first visited southern Quebec as part of a week's tour of Vermont inns. I went north on Rte. 100 from Stowe, and in what seemed a short time after driving through the small towns of Eaton Mills, Lowell and Troy, came to Newport, a very surprisingly sizable community on Lake Memphremagog. When I-91 is completed from north of Norwich, Vermont, it will eventually pass through St. Johnsbury and reach Newport. The last ten miles to the Canadian line are already completed. At Derby line I passed into Canada, picking up the Stanstead Expressway; I exited at North Hatley; then Bob Brown's excellent map gave me roads eastward to reach Lake Massawippi and Hovey Manor. It was indeed fascinating to travel in bi-lingual Quebec and perhaps it is my imagination, but there seems to be more elbow room and less commercialism than in the states. The country scenery is very fetching.

North Hatley itself proved to be a very quiet, orderly, and attractive community. There is a great deal more to it than can be seen on the surface, including the story of early settlers, who arriving in 1793, encountered wild beasts and bitter winds. Among the early settlers was Captain Ebinezer Hovey, who with Colonel Henry Cull, volunteered to take the responsibility of parceling out almost 24,000 acres of almost impenetrable forests lying along the shores of the lake.

For me, this introduction into Canadian-Quebec history proved to be a most fascinating one, and I am looking forward to increasing my knowledge and understanding of it in succeeding years with visits to North Hatley.

HOVEY MANOR, North Hatley

Bob Brown, Brandy and Alexander, the St. Bernards, and I were taking an early morning walk in mid-July. We started from the front veranda of the Manor and picked our way along the dirt roads through the maples, birches, beeches, and evergreens that led down near the lakeshore. Bob, the perfect picture of the Canadian innkeeper, pointed with his pipe to the many birds. There was a light

mist on Lake Massawippi which promised to burn off shortly after breakfast.

He was telling me about the many beautiful mansions which dot the lakeshore.

"Coincidentally," he said, "quite a few people from the American South discovered North Hatley about the turn of the century, and the Manor, along with many other houses, was built by people who built the kind of beautiful homes in which they felt most at ease. These turned out to be Southern mansions. The inn itself was built by a gentleman from Atlanta."

At this point we made a turn up onto the hardtop road, and Brandy flushed out a rabbit. A whistle from Bob brought him back, and at this point we could see five miles down the lake. There were meadows on the uphill side of the road that stretched back to the birch forest, and a hint of honeysuckle and wild flowers in the air.

We swung back onto the road leading to the Manor, and he explained: "I came up here in 1950 and have had a wonderful time ever since. There has been lots of expansion, but the important things have always been here: this beautiful, unspoiled lake, the marvelous pure air of the woods, the fishing, the wildlife, and the really wonderful people who make North Hatley their home.

"We are open year 'round," he said, "because there are five ski areas within an easy driving distance, and we have become a sort of family ski-resort as well as a family summer resort. There are also five golf courses within twenty minutes of us."

By this time we had reached the rear door of the Manor House and walked through the living room with its considerable collection of antiques which Bob and Betty have been re-finishing over the years. We passed through the great doors leading to the front terrace and decided to have breakfast out there in full view of the lake.

I found the pastoral elegance of Hovey Manor and its truly undisturbed environment impossible to resist.

HOVEY MANOR, Box 60, Rte. 10, North Hatley, Quebec, Canada; 819-842-2421. A resort-inn 85 mi. from Montreal, 35 mi. from Newport, Vt. On Lake Massawippi and near major ski areas. Lodgings. Mod. American and European Plan. Breakfast, lunch, dinner served daily. Alpine and xc ski. Bob and Betty Brown, Innkeepers.

Cape Breton, N.S.

To travel to Canada I found that I needed a small card that was an affidavit to the effect that I was a United States citizen. The border regulations are quite reasonable and a passport is not needed.

On the first trip I flew to Sidney and then proceeded by car to explore the Cabot Trail on Cape Breton. I was advised by my new friends on the Cape to do this trip both clockwise and counter-clockwise, since the scenery on both sides of the car was equally spectacular and a great deal would be missed if I only went one way.

My first trip was counter-clockwise from Baddeck across the middle of the Cape through Margaree Forks and then north through Cheticamp, Cape Rouge, Pleasant Bay, and Ingonish then back down to Bras D'or. The reverse trip was equally as exciting and it is almost like going to two different places.

The major part of Nova Scotia including Halifax and Yarmouth are on my country inn itinerary and I am sure that there will be some inns from this extremely picturesque southern Nova Scotia area in the next edition.

NORMAWAY INN, Margaree Valley

"What a beautiful morning!" June Haywood echoed all of our sentiments as she came into the sunlit dining room for breakfast.

"I just can't believe that this place really exists," she said.

The point was well made. We were far, far away from so much of the hurly-burly, and our dining room windows on both sides looked out over the golf course which surrounds this very pleasant Cape Breton inn.

The first course for breakfast was oatmeal, something near to my heart. This time it was something special, served with brown sugar and cream. Next, the salmon was brought in, fresh from the Margaree.

Fred was busy pointing out some of the points on the surrounding low mountains where Innkeeper Gerry Hart had taken us at sundown the previous evening. This visit also included a most rewarding hour at the Fish Hatchery where there were an unusual number of children "oohing" and "ahhing."

Gerry himself, the genial Boniface, came striding in the dining room, rubbing his hands together and saying, "Well, what will it be? A round of golf, or would you like to go to Lake-O-Laws and do a little fishing?" The Haywood's decided that since they had bicycled from

Baddeck they would like a day off, and so we all agreed to go fishing in the morning and perhaps play golf in the afternoon. Gerry guaranteed perfect weather for the next three days so we decided to do the Cabot Trail in its entirety the next day, and he promised a "bonny box lunch."

The Normaway is a bit of a bonny inn, itself, in the heart of the Margaree Valley which is famous for peace, tranquility and fantastic salmon fishing. It is completely surrounded by its own four hole golf course and there is a lot to do in the vicinity. It is near, but not on, the Cabot Trail.

In addition to the welcome feeling of withdrawal from the world, one of the outstanding memories I have of the Normaway is the food. It is served in heaping quantities, family-style, with one main course that is different every night.

Evenings are always enlivened by the innkeeper, who has many stories of the region. The Normaway is typical of Cape Breton hospitality. It is very informal, and I enjoyed myself tremendously with both the Canadian and USA guests.

An additional feature is the Museum of Cape Breton Heritage which is a direct outgrowth of the collection of handsome household items gathered over a period of 25 years from the homes of Cape Breton. This includes a collection of over 100 authentic tartans, maps, and notes of historic interest concerning the Cape Breton heritage. as well as a display of old-time weaving and spinning accessories brought by the Scottish immigrants over the years. There are rugs, both of the past and present, patchwork, embroideries and needlework. The Museum is open daily from June 15th until after Thanksgiving weekend. In an area where handcrafts play such an important role, it makes a very significant contribution.

As we were filing out after breakfast I heard one of the other guests say, "You know, this place is very unique."

NORMAWAY INN, Margaree Valley, Cape Breton, N.S.; 902-Margaree Forks 28. A resort inn 2 mi. east on Egypt Rd. off Cabot Trail. Lodgings. Breakfast, lunch, dinner served daily. Closed Oct. 15-June 15. Marjorie and Gerald Hart, Innkeepers.

Cape Breton natural resource

KILMUIR PLACE, Northeast Margaree

I love to get letters from Isabel Taylor. In some ways it is like hearing from people who are on a mountaintop in Tibet or in a valley in Terra del Fuego. Actually, she's in Cape Breton, Nova Scotia but there are times when Cape Breton seems to be a long way off for me. Let me share one of her letters:

"Dear Mr. Norman: (she always calls me Mr. Norman)

"I'm in my usual corner, the red chair by the window. I wish you could see the valley today. All of our trees and bushes are in full bloom, and I'm sure all of the birds are here for the summer. Ross is in the kitchen now making a couple of chocolate cakes so that he can take a few of our guests off to do some salmon fishing this afternoon. He sends his best.

"I thought of you the other day because I know how much you're affected by cooking aromas, and we had three freshly made apple pies and a mince pie that were cooling and filling the kitchen with a most marvelous feeling. Speaking of the kitchen, it has been a busy week for me because we've just finished laundering the red calico curtains in the kitchen and have done over one corner of it. We're saving your comfortable chair and a few of the Canadian magazines that you liked, as you said you were coming up here again soon."

It seems like a short season at this little family-style inn in Cape Breton. On my first visit, I talked with some people who had been coming there for a number of years and then built their own houses in the vicinity. This is one of the great salmon fishing areas of the world, and there is a little salmon museum (which I found very informative) just up the road a short way from the Kilmuir

Place. Naturally, everyone up here is concerned about preserving the salmon streams.

This is a very tiny American Plan inn with five or
six lodging rooms, booked well in advance. Everybody
eats at a big dining room table with rather elegant appointments. In addition to salmon and all of its variations,
Isabel sets a table that includes roast beef, steak, lamb
and lobster.

While they ordinarily do not take people off the
highway as far as meals are concerned, she did take some
advance reservations saying, "If I know they are coming,
we can handle them if there are not too many in the
party."

*KILMUIR PLACE, Northeast Margaree, Cape Breton,
N.S.; 902-Margaree Forks 26. A country inn 28 mi. from
Baddeck on the Cabot Trail. Mod. American Plan. Lodg-
ings. Breakfast, lunch, dinner served daily. Open May —
September. Mr. and Mrs. Ross Taylor, Innkeepers.*

INVERARY INN, Baddeck

Isobel MacAulay and I strolled down the road back
of the Inverary Inn through the evergreens to the
shores of Loch Bras D'or. "It means," she explained,
"literally an arm of gold." I was immediately struck by
the resemblance of the scene in Cape Breton to the shores
of New York State's Finger Lakes and also to the eastern
shores of Lake Michigan at Leelanau.

"Oh, we Scots have a deep heritage here," she said,
as a bit of a burr crept into her speech. "Most of the
people in our village here in
Baddeck are either Camp-
bells or MacDonalds and
most of our fathers or grandfathers originally came from
Scotland." I asked whether
or not they might be Scottish
first and Canadian second.
"Well, we're Canadian," she
said, "except on certain Scot
holidays and during the Scottish Mod."

As we reached the shores
of this beautifully crystal

Church near Inverary Inn

239

clear, totally unspoiled lake, I picked up one of the small warm stones and skipped it out across the water. We came upon a small boathouse and sat down with our backs against the warm boards just to take in the whole scene.

"Oh," she said, "you should see it here in the Fall. Everything breaks into a full blaze. Well, now that I've shown you the way, I've got to get back to meet some guests that I expect this morning. You'll be coming in for lunch, won't you?" I assured her that I indeed would.

She left me to the quietude, the high hills, the blue sky and the scudding clouds. Sailboats were out this morning, and down the lake a couple of fishermen were quietly stalking some of our finny friends.

The Inverary Inn is named for a Scottish village. It is very clean, homey and quite informal. While there, I met some other guests from the states that had been coming for quite a few consecutive years. Besides the Cabot Trail, which is the spectacular road around the Cape, they had several other suggestions about side trips for me. The accommodations, which include rooms in the inn and also several adjacent cottages, are pleasantly rustic. There are no televisions or telephones, but several Canadian and British books and magazines are about. The dining room, with its gorgeous view of the Loch, has good, hearty Nova Scotia food including freshly caught Nova Scotia salmon and it is served in a variety of pleasing ways.

I shook myself from my reverie and decided to take the long walk back to the inn and then go to the Alexander Graham Bell Museum before lunch. I wondered, as I set off through the pine trees, and stopped for a moment to watch the fish jumping through the sun be-dazzled surface of the lake, whether that was a skirl of bagpipes I heard, or just my own Scottish imagination getting the better of me.

INVERARY INN, Box 190, Baddick, Cape Breton, N.S.; 902-295-2674. A village inn 52 mi. from Sidney, N.S. on the shores of Bras D'or Lakes. 1 mi. east of Trans-Canada Hgwy. Lodgings. Breakfast, lunch, dinner served daily. Closed Oct. 15 — June 1st. Isobel MacAulay, Innkeeper.